PUPPY
PROBLEMS

THE DOG'S-EYE
VIEW ON CARING
FOR YOUR PET

PUPPY PROBLEMS

THE DOG'S-EYE VIEW ON CARING FOR YOUR PET

SOPHIE COLLINS

AMMONITE
PRESS

First published 2019 by
Ammonite Press
an imprint of Guild of Master Craftsman Publications Ltd
Castle Place, 166 High Street, Lewes,
East Sussex, BN7 1XU
United Kingdom
www.ammonitepress.com

ISBN 978 1 78145 335 3

Publisher: Jason Hook
Design Manager: Robin Shields
Editor: Jamie Pumfrey
Photographer: Neil Grundy
Designer: Wayne Blades
Retouching and Cutouts: Jon Hoag and Alex Bailey

Colour reproduction by GMC Reprographics
Printed and bound in Turkey

CONTENTS

INTRODUCTION

WHERE IT ALL STARTS

If you've always thought that puppyhood was something to be waited out, and that the cuddly, non-stop-playing-and-peeing little creature you just brought home will simply evolve into the pet of your dreams without too much work, you were wrong. Waiting is part of it, of course, and no matter how a puppy is treated, growing up will bring some changes. But just like a new person would, he needs to learn the way things work from you. And since he isn't a person, but a different species, you need to find ways to direct him onto the right path, and help him to understand you – and, along the way, hopefully, vice versa. From the moment you carried your puppy to the car, you became his all-knowing window on the world. And, as with any other important undertaking, you need to have a plan.

AH, A PLAN!

Having a plan doesn't necessarily mean raising a puppy should be run like a military operation (though there are times when that might help). But it does mean thinking ahead and being aware of how things might seem to your puppy, as well as how they look to you. Taking a puppy-level view will help you understand why he loves what he loves, what things might scare him (and how you can help him overcome his fears), and why he does the things you'd prefer he didn't do (so you can come up with kind, constructive ways to get him to stop). He's small and he can't explain himself – or at least not in language you can yet understand – so it's up to you to make it all work.

Planning also means that you have the things you need when you need them. It avoids any unnecessary wringing of hands over the latest chewed lead, phone or shoes (although every new puppy will chew something he shouldn't at some point in the first few days, because no new owner can ever believe the extent to which they're going to have to learn to put things away). It also smooths the way for some of the skills such as house-training or walking on the lead that will take time and, on your part, patience, for him to master.

Note: There's a tradition of referring to the dog as 'he' in dog books, and we've stuck with it for reasons of clarity – except when the subject of the text is specifically female.

▼ Freshly minted
Cheerful, energetic and amusing, a new puppy can be a pleasure. But if it's a long time since you last had one at home, you may have forgotten that he can be challenging, too.

The good news is that puppies are usually very willing to try to see life through a person's eyes. Dogs have become our top companion species largely because they're excellent at reading people, often to the point where they seem to be able to second-guess what we're going to do next. It's a rare dog that doesn't spend a large part of the day carefully watching his owners and wondering what they're going to do next. So your puppy is pretty likely to have the raw material you need to work with already in place. All you need to do is learn how to use it to create the relationship you want with your pet.

▼ **Look and learn**

From the time he's a tiny puppy all the way up to adulthood, your dog will be your closest observer. If you watch him equally closely, you'll find that you learn a huge amount about both his personality and his behaviour.

PUPPY PROBLEMS

DOG'S-EYE VIEW

HOW IT WORKS

Throughout this book you'll find 'Dog's-eye view' boxes. These take into account the way in which I, your dog, may see things. They will help to demonstrate that there are always at least two sides to any situation: mine and yours! After all, the easiest way to persuade someone else to come around to your way of seeing things is to recognize the way they see things themselves. And that goes for me, too!

UNDERSTANDING YOUR PUPPY'S VIEWPOINT

Your puppy may not be able to speak, but the better you get to know him, the easier you'll find it to 'read' him. And as you get used to watching him for clues, you'll also stop making assumptions about what different behaviours mean. Did you know, for example, that a lot of yawning may signify that he's nervous, not tired? Or that his attempts to jump up near your face are more likely to be a sign of deference towards you than an expression of cheek?

The dog's-eye view boxes included in the text offer insights into your puppy's perspective and explain some of his needs and likes. Why it is that he likes chewing so much, for instance, or what it is that's so scary about the vacuum cleaner? Or why does it always seems to be so much easier for him to start doing something than to stop?

If you learn to look at things from your puppy's own viewpoint (or, given that you're only human, as close to it as you can manage), then you'll also develop a better sense of how you should approach any issues that arise.

Over the last two decades, as research into domestic dogs has become fashionable, we've learned far, far more about canine cognition: the way in which our pets work and think. One of the welcome results of this has been a re-appraisal of the relationship between dog and owner – today, the thinking is that the best relationship you can have with your dog is one of teamwork, rather than master-and-servant. And the earlier you start, the stronger the team you and your puppy will make.

▼ **Not so tired**
A yawning adolescent may be nervous rather than sleepy. Learn to recognize canine body language, and it'll put you a step ahead in the puppy behaviour stakes.

CHAPTER ONE

BRAND **NEW**

Are you just thinking about getting a puppy? Or have you already found him, and are waiting until he's old enough to bring home? Or perhaps he is already ensconced on your sofa and busy chewing his first toy? Whichever is the case, this chapter can help. It takes you through the key things you need to know, from choosing a puppy to puppy-proofing your home, and what to expect on his first day – and night. Read it through to avoid unwelcome surprises and give yourself a head start on the first few days.

WHERE'S YOUR PUPPY
COMING FROM?

Where is your puppy coming from? A breeder or a rescue centre? If you're so organized that you're reading this book ahead of deciding, read this page first; if you've already bought your puppy, read it anyway so that you can help advise other potential dog owners.

BREEDER

If you want to buy from a breeder, read up as much as you can in advance. You need to find out about any breed-specific or inherited health concerns, and to visit in order to see the mother and puppies before you commit. Reputable breeders won't mind answering a lot of questions; they'll take your interest as a sign that you will be a good owner.

If your initial contact results in an offer to meet you with a puppy somewhere nearby 'to save you the drive', or your suggestion that you see the puppies with their mother in the home seems to be problematic, don't buy. The likelihood in

these cases is that what's being presented as a home-bred situation is a cover for farmed puppies (see below).

When you do visit, what you want to see in a home situation is a safe, warm place for the mother and puppies in a not-too sterile environment – the richer the environment puppies find themselves in, the better for them. A sterile, tiled space that has no variety of textures and scents for a growing puppy to explore isn't as beneficial for him as a messier-looking arrangement such as a pen with newspaper, blankets and toys that is set up in a corner of a utility room or kitchen.

◄ Let your head lead
An adorable line-up of puppies may elicit an 'aww' response, but make sure you read up on both breeds and sources carefully before you go ahead with a new puppy. Remember, it's a relationship that may last as long as 16 or so years, so it's worth getting right.

PUPPY PROBLEMS

► **Check your source**
If you want to rescue a dog but would prefer a puppy rather than an older dog, approach some breed-specific rescues: they may be able to offer a puppy which is also a rescue dog.

RESCUE ORGANIZATIONS

Contrary to what you may have been told, you can get a puppy through rescue organizations, and by going to a breed-specific rescue, you may be able to find a puppy of the breed you want. Research local rescues online and then visit them – most centres will be happy for you to do some volunteer dog walking, which will give you a feel for how they operate. A breed-specific rescue may be further away but, again, you can do a lot of research online. Most rescues will insist on an undertaking to neuter when the puppy is old enough (they see too many of the results of uncontrolled breeding), and will ask for a donation towards their costs.

PET STORE AND ONLINE ADVERTISING

Two words: don't buy. Puppies in pet stores have almost without exception come from puppy farms, and you don't want to do anything to support this horrible business. Steps are being taken in the UK to ban puppy farms and pet shop sales, but it will be a while before they become illegal. Breeding bitches in puppy farms are often kept in terrible conditions, in small and insanitary cages, and bred from every season – the battery hens of the dog world, they have no quality of life at all. The puppies they produce are bred purely for profit, and no attention is paid to their early developmental needs. Many online advertisements, too, originate with puppy farms. A lot of the puppies will have life-long temperament and health problems resulting from their impoverished start in life.

IF YOU'VE ALREADY BOUGHT...

What if you already have a puppy from a pet store, or you bought one online without realizing the implications? Think positive, undertake to give them the best life they can possibly have, and let others know about the puppy-farm trade (and the ways in which it's often masked or disguised). It will be impossible to stop such a profitable business until it's more widely known about, and shunned.

WHICH BREED
OF PUPPY?

It may seem to be a bit of a downer, when your immediate interest is in the sweetest sort of puppy you might have, but it is really important to think through the practicalities of owning a dog, both long- and short-term. It's far better to do this now than further down the line, when you realize you hadn't really factored in the realities of owning a puppy, or the adult dog he'll grow into.

PUG OR POINTER?

Think about what you can offer before you get too fixed on a specific breed of puppy. Be honest about how much exercise you're prepared to do (one hour's walking daily? Two hours?) and how much time you can spend with a puppy. If you work all week and come home tired in the evening, getting a puppy or even an adult dog isn't such a good idea – they don't just switch off when you go to work, and it's not recommended that any dog, much less a puppy, be left for longer than four hours at a time. Consider, too, your circumstances – how big your home is, whether or not you have a garden and so on.

LEARN YOUR BREEDS

Read up on the dogs you feel are options, but don't dismiss breeds you haven't thought of yet, and don't get too hung up on specific looks or characteristics. You may be surprised, for example, if you have a busy life, that a whippet or greyhound is worth considering, – although they need full-on, off-lead exercise, it may only be for as little as 30 minutes a day, after which they are happy to lie around for much of the time. Contrast that with terrier breeds – many much smaller and, you might think, less demanding – who will not only need substantially longer walks but also to be kept busy for much of their downtime. Check any genetic tendencies towards particular health conditions in different breeds, too; vet bills and insurance can be expensive. And remember to think long term – your puppy will turn into a dog who may live for anything from eight to 10 years (larger breeds) to 10 to 16 (smaller ones).

WHEN YOU MEET

Sometimes you'll be offered a choice of puppies. How do you choose? You want a confident, relaxed puppy, so sit down on the floor and watch how they behave.

A curious puppy who comes straight to you may be a better bet than a shy one, who hangs back. If you gently pick a puppy up, what does he do? Great if he wriggles happily, trying to get closer to your face (as he would with an adult dog). Not so good if he shows any signs of fear (eyes wide, ears flat), or seems to be concentrating on how to get away.

Lastly, what if you – again, gently – roll a puppy on his back and lightly hold him there for a second or two. Good if he submits in a relaxed, unworried way; less good if he's clearly unhappy being restrained, however lightly, and struggles hard.

BODY LANGUAGE

Even small puppies express themselves quite clearly. When you're meeting several, bear in mind what kind of home you can offer (Busy? Small kids? Calm and quiet? Dog-centred?) and what kind of canine personality will fit in best.

If he stays relaxed when you gently roll him over, it's a good sign.

A very timid, back-hanging puppy is likely to need more support as he develops.

A confident puppy who's happy to embrace new experiences may be your best choice.

BREED CHARACTERISTICS

The idea that particular breeds have specific characteristics has a good deal of truth in it, but it dates from the era when all dogs were working dogs and only those that were best suited to whatever their job was would be bred from. This is what created retrievers who retrieve and herding dogs that herd. Today, when being a retriever, say, doesn't necessarily mean that your puppy comes hardwired to retrieve, his personality and its suitability for his life as a pet are likely to count for more in the long term.

THINGS
YOU NEED

How prepared do you need to be for a puppy? You need to be aware of how much care and attention the new family member will need, but a new puppy doesn't require lots of possessions. Although it's tempting to buy everything imaginable on the 'you might need' list, it makes more sense to buy the bare minimum and wait until your puppy arrives to add to it. Different puppies have different needs and you may find, for example, that having stocked up on what everyone has assured you is the 'perfect' food, it doesn't seem to suit your puppy.

WHAT YOU NEED

Here's a short list of the immediate essentials, plus another list of things to consider when the puppy has settled in a little.

STRAIGHT AWAY

- **Something from 'home'**
  Your puppy's sense of smell is so acute that the best comforter for him is anything that smells of the home he's just left (and of his mother and siblings). This should be fabric – a piece of blanket or towel, a small stuffed toy or anything else that has spent time in the puppy pen. Most breeders will offer something; if not, ask.

- **Collar and harness**
  You'll need a soft, adjustable fabric collar with a tag, and a harness (ask the breeder for a size estimate, as you'll want to take these with you to collect him). In the early days of teaching him to walk 'with' you, a harness may be the easiest way to keep him alongside without straining his neck as he wanders around. The tag should have your surname, phone number and address on it.

- **Food**
  Ask the breeder what the puppy was weaned on, and what he's eating now. Even if you have a feeding 'system' in mind (Raw feeding? Kibble? Home-cooked?), it's best to keep his food the same while he's settling in, and to change it gradually if you want to, to avoid stomach upsets during his first days with you. You will also need food and water bowls; ceramic or stainless steel is best.

- **Something to sleep in**
  In the short term, this can be anything from a purpose-made puppy bed to a well-lined and cosy cardboard box – your puppy won't mind which, so long as it is warm and comfortable.

- **Crate**
  Unless you are certain you *don't* want to use a crate, buy one that is the right size before your puppy comes home. It needs to be big enough for him to stand up and easily turn around in. If you want it to last longer, bigger crates with dividers are available, so that you can use a smaller space to start with and remove the divider as he grows.

- **Toy**
  A small, sturdy soft toy or rope toy for him to chew on, possibly one that can double up as a tug toy, is the best bet (avoid hard squeaky toys for now – he may remove and swallow the 'squeak').

- **Old towels and blankets**
  You'll need plenty of soft, washable fabric from day one – to line beds, dry off a muddy puppy, and protect upholstery.

IN THE LONGER TERM

- **A seatbelt for the car**
  If he's going to travel on the seat. Otherwise, a travel crate to go in the back.

- **A long line**
  To use around the house and garden when you want him to enjoy some freedom, but still be able to keep tabs on him.

- **A permanent bed**
  If you've been using the cardboard-box option in the short term.

- **Soft grooming brush**
  This is to get him used to the idea of being brushed gently.

DON'T PRE-BUY

- **Masses of toys**
  Some toys aren't suitable for a very young puppy, and you don't know what he prefers to play with yet.

If you avoid over-shopping at first, you'll soon establish the must-haves and the don't-really-needs for your new puppy.

HOW TO
PUPPY PROOF

Puppy-proofing your space is the single thing that will make your and your puppy's lives much easier during his first week or two. Done thoroughly, it will mean that he stays safe while you get into a routine together (and embark on house-training).

FIVE WAYS TO KEEP YOUR PUPPY OUT OF TROUBLE:

1   Keep all plugs and leads out of a puppy's way. This can be a challenge: block them off behind piles of books or boxes, or use a lead caddy to wind all the leads into one place and guard them from puppy teeth. Remember to unplug any electrical appliances, wind up the leads and leave on a high surface when you're leaving the room. A love of chewing electric leads seems to be one thing that all puppies have in common.

2   Think about where your puppy will be safe and where you might sometimes need to keep him out. A child gate or two will be useful for when you need him to stay in one safe place (the kitchen?) for half an hour; or when you don't want him to go upstairs and so on. Some owners use a child's play pen to keep their puppy corralled where they can see him at times when they can't supervise.

▼ **Think small**
Tidy up all electric flexes, not just the visible ones. A small puppy may well be able to wriggle into forgotten spaces – behind your computer, say, or the back of the fridge.

STAY IN VIEW

Even if you're busy and need me out from underfoot, I prefer it if I can see you: if you put me behind a stairgate, I may whimper and whine a bit, but I can still see what's going on, and I feel more secure. Hearing you isn't as reassuring for me as seeing you, which is why I hate it so much when you shut the door.

▼ Rubbish collector

Bins often represent an irresistible attraction to puppies: they offer a rich variety of smells and, if upended, tastes and textures, too. So guard yours well, even if it means weighting it down, while he's still young.

3 Puppies love remote controls and mobile phones; for a while, keep a basket or a shoebox up high in each room and get used to putting anything with obvious puppy appeal in it as you leave the room.

4 Pick up shoes and other items that are likely to be good chew-value, and leave them behind closed doors. Make sure your puppy exits the room when you do and shut the door behind you both.

5 Keep your rubbish out of reach. If you don't already have one, a heavyweight rubbish bin in the kitchen may be a good investment: emptying the trash is a popular puppy pastime.

Remember, the puppy stage is not for ever. As your puppy gets older, and provided you keep him busy and occupied, he'll get used to what he's allowed to play with and what's off limits. In the meantime, making sure that anything not allowed isn't accessible will pay off.

COLLECTING
YOUR PUPPY

In the past, puppies tended to be taken to their new homes when they were eight weeks old. Gradually, though, research has revealed the importance of a puppy's early socialization period and as a result, a puppy is sometimes taken to his new home slightly younger, at around six weeks.

The key socialization period is generally judged to last from when a puppy is four weeks old to when he reaches 16 weeks (see pages 34–35). In terms of adjustment and learning, it's the most important time of his life: the period during which he absorbs his world and everything in it. A puppy that sees and experiences as much as possible during this time, in a positive, fear-free environment is well set up for becoming a well-adjusted dog. Many owners prefer to collect their puppy at six weeks in order for him to experience as much of the socialization period as possible in his long-term home.

THE PRACTICALITIES OF GETTING HIM HOME

You'll probably be making some kind of journey to collect your new puppy, whether this is a short car ride or a lengthy drive. If you need to make a long trip, prepare the car to be as comfortable as possible for your puppy. It may be easiest if you take someone with you, so they can deal with the puppy on the back seat while you drive. But if you don't have a travel companion, your puppy can travel in a deep cardboard box lined with towels, or in a crate – whichever is the easiest for you to arrange.

▶ **A safe pair of hands**
Carry your puppy securely, with a hand under his bottom and another around his chest. Bear in mind small puppies are great escape artists, so make sure your arrangements will keep him safe on his first car journey.

When you pick your puppy up, remember to ask for:

- Something that will smell of 'home' to settle him in. This can be a small piece of blanket or towel or a soft toy: anything that's been around his mother and siblings and that will have absorbed their smell.
- Any breed papers or vaccination certificates.
- Details of the food he's been weaned onto, and his current feeding routine – both the timing of his meals and the amount he's fed.

If it's a long trip and you're travelling solo, plan in regular breaks and take water and a bowl for your puppy. He may be car-sick (many puppies are during their first car rides) so bring an old towel or two for mopping up. Remember that if he needs a break from the car, you may have to bring a collar and lead (and he'll be unused to both) or carry him, then put him down carefully supervised for a minute or two in a safe place. Try to avoid anywhere that's used as a general dog lavatory (for example, the verges at service stations on the motorway), because these areas will be risky to him until he's had his vaccinations. Instead, aim to stop off somewhere that won't be much used by other dogs.

▲ **Something familiar**
If at all possible, bring at least one familiar object home with your puppy (and if you're offered more than one, accept). He'll be just as content with a piece of old blanket or towel as he will with a toy: the whole point of it is the way it smells, which will offer reassurance in his new surroundings.

COLLECTING YOUR PUPPY

THE FIRST
NIGHT

Your puppy's first night may be a disturbed one – both for him and for you. The busy day and the journey to his new home will probably have distracted him from the parting from his family, but at night he'll find himself sleeping alone for the first time, and he may find it hard to settle. Spend some time playing with him before his final trip outdoors, so that when bedtime comes he's already tired.

SETTLING DOWN

In the past, puppies were often expected to tough it out when it came to the first few nights. Today, it's no longer regarded as spoiling your puppy to take extra care to settle him in gently. There aren't any advantages to his being unhappy, and you can do a lot to build the bond between you if you make this first night or two easier for him.

Decide ahead where your puppy is going to sleep, but don't shut him so far away that you can't hear him cry. Many people, even if they don't ultimately want their dog to sleep in the bedroom, opt to have their puppy in the room with them for the first few nights. If you're not going down the crate route, you can improvise with a deep cardboard box that he's unlikely to be able to climb out of. Line the crate or box with newspaper, overlaid with plenty of soft blankets or towels. This is the time to take out the piece of blanket from his first home too. Tuck it into his improvised bed – its familiar smell will comfort him. If it's a chilly night, fill a hot-water bottle with hot (not boiling) water, wrap it up well in another blanket and put that in his bed.

Take him out for a last wee, and settle him down in his bed. If he cries, soothe him in a calm voice, but don't rush over and take him out to comfort him. On the other hand, if you hear a lot of whining and scrabbling during the night, chances are that he needs to go out. Don't leave him to soil his crate or box; get up and take him outside (you may as well get a headstart on house-training, unwelcome though middle-of-the-night trips to the garden may be), praise him when he performs, then bring him in again. Be firm about putting him back to bed when you get in, and keep up the soothing-words routine if necessary. Even if you have a disturbed night, your puppy is still likely to sleep for much of it because he will be tired out after a long day.

MY DAY OF CHANGES

It was the busiest day I've ever had: first I met new people, then they put me in a car (my first ever ride), and I was sick, then we got somewhere altogether new and I ran around. The garden is good, and there are lots of brand-new smells in the house. Then I had my supper and played for a while. And then I was sleepy, and everyone went to bed, and it was the first time that I realized that my mother and brothers and sisters weren't there, and I felt lonely so I cried. One of the new people sat by my crate and talked to me quietly, though, and eventually I went back to sleep on my bit of blanket. It smells of my dog family.

▼ Sleeping arrangements
Whether you decide on a crate or a basket, try to make sure your puppy stays in it for his first night. You may need to get up to let him out once or twice, but unless you're happy to have him sleep with you forever, don't take him onto the bed with you: if you do, he'll expect to sleep there from that point on.

THE FIRST
DAY

You've got your new puppy home, you survived the first night and it's his first day with you. The biggest surprise for a brand new owner, especially if this is your first puppy or if it's a long time since you last had a dog, is quite how much work it is keeping an eight- to 10-week-old puppy safe, fed and entertained (as well as getting enough rest), while simultaneously getting going on house-training, and doing anything else. Whoever said a puppy was less work than a baby?

HOW DOES THE DAY LOOK?

It may seem picky to divide a puppy's first day into half-hour slots, but this timetable will give you an idea of what life with a very small puppy entails. The real surprise for those without much young-puppy experience will be the half-hourly trips outside. Some suggest once an hour will be enough, but the more opportunities you give your puppy to 'perform' outside, reinforced with praise for doing so, the sooner the house-training penny will drop for him. And very small puppies don't have much bladder control – when they need to go, they go. Of course, you don't have to stay outside long – give your puppy the opportunity to go and if nothing happens, come back indoors and try again a short time later.

▼ Accidents will happen

Be prepared – even a puppy who's fast on the uptake will have some accidents. When it happens, clear up without making a fuss and use a petshop product made for the purpose – it won't smell of ammonia, which is found in most ordinary cleaning products, and the smell of which can encourage him to go in the same spot again.

DOG'S-EYE VIEW

AN ALL-NEW WORLD

This new place is full of things to do; I spent most of the morning sniffing and snuffling around, playing with smaller humans (they've given me a raggy thing to play tug with), peeing (both inside and out), and rushing around the garden. It's exhausting, though: I find that I fall asleep every so often, then, when I wake up, I start all over again. Although sometimes I forget where I am for a moment or two and rush around the room like crazy, and my new humans have to give me downtime so I can calm down.

SETTING UP A SCHEDULE

You'll find more on this on pages 30–31, but this gives you an idea of just how often a two-month old puppy will need pee breaks. If you can get him outside at least once an hour – and keep an especially sharp eye on him just after he's woken up, straight after he's eaten and when he's been playing hard, you're most likely to catch the moment before an accident happens. This sample schedule also shows three mealtimes but some eight-week puppies are still eating four meals spread across the day.

6.30am	Wake up; take outside for toileting
7.00am	First meal
7.30am	Back outside for toileting
8.00am	Playtime
8.30am	Outside for toileting
9.00am	Rest time
9.30am	Outside for toileting
10.00am	Short session of handling/grooming with a soft brush
10.30am	Outside for toileting
11.00am	Quiet time
11.30am	Outside for toileting
12.00 noon	Second meal
12.30pm	Outside for toileting
1.00pm	Rest time
1.30pm	Outside for toileting
2.00pm	Playtime
2.30pm	Outside for toileting
3.00pm	Start puppy training
3.30pm	Outside for toileting
4.00pm	Rest time
4.30pm	Outside for toileting
5.00pm	Third meal
5.30pm	Outside for toileting
6.00pm	Mixing time – with the family as a group
6.30pm	Outside for toileting
7.00pm	Winding down – quiet play
7.30pm	Last visit outside before bed
8.00pm	Bedtime

WHAT ARE THE
EATING OPTIONS?

It's often said that we are what we eat, and this is also true for your puppy. So it's worth making sure that he's getting good nutrition from the start and putting some thought into how you want to feed him in the long term.

WHAT TO FEED YOUR PUPPY?

Begin by feeding him the same food that he was weaned onto (you may have been given some to take home with you). If you want to change his meals, do it gradually – swap one-third of each meal for the new food for a day or two, then serve a 50/50 mix for another day or two, before finally feeding complete meals of the new food.

PUPPY FOOD?

Does an eight-week puppy need to eat a different kind of food from a grown-up dog? Broadly, his nutritional needs are higher – he needs a higher percentage of protein, fat and some minerals than adult dogs do – so he should either be fed branded food specifically for puppies, or, if you're planning to feed home-cooked or raw, you should take advice from your vet to make sure he'll be getting everything he needs. Large breeds require

▼ **Keep it familiar**
A newly arrived puppy should eat the food that he's used to for a few days at least. Everything else around him has changed, so the food he's getting should be familiar, while he gets used to his new surroundings.

PUPPY PROBLEMS

extra consideration, as they need to grow at a steady, rather than speedy, rate to avoid stressing their joints (which can show up in adult dogs as hip dysplasia and other joint problems). So you may be recommended a specific food that takes this into account.

The age at which a puppy transfers to adult food also varies – the rule of thumb is that the switch happens when they've grown to about three-quarters of their adult size. In smaller breeds that's usually at around nine months; with medium-sized dogs it's around a year; and larger or giant breeds may be around 16 months old before they move to an adult diet.

You can feed your puppy commercial food, or home-cook for him, or, more unusually, take the raw food option. Whole books have been written on all three, but the same food won't suit every puppy. Some general information follows, but it should be stressed that initial advice on your puppy's diet should come from his breeder and your vet, as it's crucial that he gets the right balance of nutrients while he's still growing.

▼ How much?

Again, a breeder or vet will advise on how much food your puppy should be getting, and how much to increase it as he grows. You want him to be getting plenty of calories and nutrients, but you'll also want to ensure he stays lean and healthy.

READ THE LABEL

Commercial foods vary a lot; some are substantially better than others. Ignore all claims (and pictures) on the packaging. The only words that matter are in the ingredients list, so learn to micro-read the label. Generally a short list of recognizable ingredients indicates a better food. Vague labelling and a long list of less recognizable ingredients are best avoided. Foods with added colouring or that contain sugars should be bypassed too – neither are either necessary or desirable in dog food. The meat element of the food, ideally over 60 per cent, should come first in the list, and the other elements should describe specific foods rather than food groups.
So, for example:
- 'Chicken', 'lamb' or 'beef', for example, are better than 'meat and animal derivatives' (the latter can mean any part of any animal)
- 'Rice' or 'potato starch' are better than 'cereals'
- 'Sunflower oil' is better than 'oils'
and so on.

COMMERCIAL FOOD

This comes in dry or wet varieties – that is, either kibble or biscuit, or wetter meaty mixtures in tins or trays. The chances are that your puppy will have been weaned onto one or other variety of commercial food, and that will be what he's eating when he arrives home with you. Commercial food remains the most popular choice when it comes to feeding pet dogs.

Pros: It's convenient and your puppy is probably already used to it.

Cons: The ingredients used in commercial food for dogs can range from good to appalling (see box on page 27), so you need to make sure that you choose one of the good options. High levels of additives, in particular, can make a puppy hyper.

HOME-COOKED

If you want to know exactly what your puppy is eating, you may opt to give him a home-cooked diet. There are plenty of guides available, both in book form and online, to ensure you give him the right balance of fat, protein, carbohydrate, fibre and minerals.

Pros: You can give your pet a varied, balanced diet with a full awareness of exactly what he's eating.

Cons: Preparing meals yourself can be time-consuming and expensive if you're picky about the ingredients.

▼ Happy chewing
Puppies not only enjoy it, they also need to chew as their teeth come through. There are some suggestions for chewing choices on pages 42–43.

PUPPY PROBLEMS

RAW

Raw or BARF (Bones And Raw Food) diets tend to divide opinion: owners who swear by them as the most natural way to feed a dog, and those who worry about diseases in raw meat and are concerned that the diet is not healthy. They're based on the way that a dog would naturally eat in the wild. You can buy and prepare the raw ingredients yourself or get ready-made packs of raw food from a supplier.

Pros: The high bone content often benefits a dog's teeth and digestion. Waste is drier and less smelly. Some behaviourists believe that feeding raw can be helpful with behavioural problems.

Cons: Some vets have reservations about the benefits of raw diets, and they can be messy to prepare, unless you opt for one of the pre-prepared commercial raw foods.

WARNING

FOODS DOGS CAN'T EAT

Most people know that dogs should never be given chocolate (it contains theobromine, which they can't digest). But there's a longer list of foods, below, that your puppy (indeed, any dog) shouldn't have. In some cases it's known why these foods are toxic to dogs. In others (for example, grapes, raisins and macadamia nuts), although we know they can make dogs very ill, we don't know why.

- Avocados (they contain persin, which is toxic for dogs)
- Dairy products, other than cheese. Adult dogs are lactose-intolerant, and your puppy will be able to tolerate lactose less and less as he gets older
- Grapes and raisins
- Macadamia nuts
- Onions
- Any food containing xylitol, an artificial sweetener found in chewing gum, many sweets, and toothpaste. It causes low blood sugar and liver damage; even a small amount can kill a puppy.

PEEING AND
MORE PEEING

House-training isn't usually particularly difficult – some puppies grasp the principle quickly, while it takes others a bit longer – but if you want it to happen efficiently, you, or a friend or family member, need to be in the immediate vicinity of your puppy pretty much full-time while he's learning. You need to remember to get him outside at least every hour or ideally every half-hour, offering lavish praise when they perform, and quickly and quietly clearing up any accidents indoors (using a purpose-made product, not an ammonia-based one).

AT HOME

While you're in the house with your puppy, he needs to be in your vision so that you can take him straight outside if you spot the signs he needs to go, in between his – already very frequent – scheduled trips outside. Alternatively, he should be in a confined space – this might be in the kitchen or a utility room, but he should also be behind a gate, or in a play pen, or in his crate (if you use one). Limiting his 'roaming' space will mean that he's less likely to wee unnoticed in a corner, and you'll be aware if any accidents have happened.

CRATE-TRAINING

Dogs, even when they're very young, have a 'den' mentality – that is, they don't like to dirty their sleeping space. Crate-training a puppy uses this dislike by first encouraging the puppy to see the crate as his den, and then confining him here for short periods in order to facilitate house-training.

▼ Heading out
House-training begins with your puppy understanding that peeing should happen outdoors, so make sure to reinforce him every single time he gets it right.

If you want to use your crate as a house-training aid, start by giving your puppy positive associations with it – make it warm and cosy, put toys and treats in it, wait until he's happy to go there for downtime or a nap before ever shutting the door. When he's already going to his crate and settling happily, practise shutting the door for just a minute, then opening it again.

Build on this very gradually until he's happy to be in his crate for a while with the door shut. It's not possible to be specific about exact times, but err on the short side: if you leave him in there, with his very limited bladder control, and he ends up having to pee, you've undone the exercise. The ideal is to put him into his crate after he's been outside so you can leave him for a 'safe' 20 minutes or so, then let him out and take him straight outside, where he'll pee again and be praised for it.

SPOTTING THE SIGNS

Puppies can't hold their pee for very long – he needs to go when:

- He starts turning circles
- He starts intently sniffing the ground
- He's just been let out after being behind a stairgate or in his crate
- He's just eaten
- He's been playing energetically
- He's glancing at the door
- He's wandered off from the toy he was chewing.

Ideally he'll already be outside 'to schedule' before he shows the signs, but if you see any of the above, clap your hands to get his attention and run outside with him. Don't pick him up in your enthusiasm to avoid an accident – let him run there with you.

▼ Snuffling about
Almost all puppies will snuffle about and circle before squatting. If you're quick enough, you'll be able to get him outside before the inevitable happens. And shortly he'll start to look to you to let him out when he knows he needs to pee.

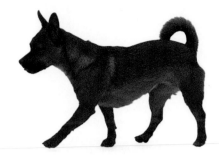

▲ **Learning from friends**
Use any socialization opportunities with older canine friends to reinforce house-training too. Puppies usually look to adult dogs to learn how to behave, so play dates can double-up as lessons in when and where to pee.

OUTSIDE

When you're outside with your puppy, walk around with him and stay outside – don't go back in the house without him, or he'll simply want to follow. Of course, there will be times when you're playing outside anyway, and he has to go. If that happens, praise him in exactly the same way as you would if you had brought him out specially – he's learning that going indoors doesn't pay a dividend or get any special attention, while going outdoors always has a positive result. And because dogs tend to go in the same spots, the more often he goes outside, the more likely he is to do it outside next time.

ACCIDENTS

There will be accidents with even the fastest learner. Don't express any displeasure, even with your body language: if your puppy spots or senses it, it's more likely to make him pee in a 'secret' corner next time, so he won't displease you.

HOW LONG WILL IT TAKE?

The rules sound – are – simple, but it's the relentlessness of house-training that can make it seem arduous, especially if your puppy is at the slower end of the scale. There's a reason why there are a number of bestsellers with titles like 'House-train your puppy in a week', but that's not a realistic promise. Most puppies will get the idea within a month or two, but you can expect accidents to happen for several months more.

TIME INDOORS

While he's being house-trained it makes sense to limit the available indoor area. Block off upstairs by using a stairgate, and stick mainly to one or two rooms – perhaps the kitchen and utility room? The larger the space available to him, the harder it will be for him to 'get' the differentiation between indoors and outdoors. If he's in any other rooms, make sure you're right by him, ready to get him outside if necessary.

PUPPY PROOFING

A couple of stairgates are invaluable while you're house-training to keep him out of specific areas when you can't have your puppy under constant watch. You can give him free range when you're with him. Many owners find it helps to keep a housetraining puppy on a single floor, to avoid him repeat-peeing in unseen corners away from you, and you can move the gates around to suit you on an hour-to-hour basis.

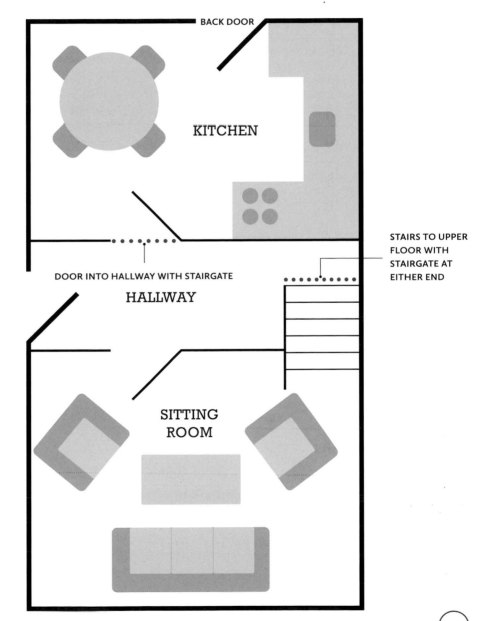

BACK DOOR

KITCHEN

STAIRS TO UPPER FLOOR WITH STAIRGATE AT EITHER END

DOOR INTO HALLWAY WITH STAIRGATE

HALLWAY

SITTING ROOM

THE WIDER
WORLD

By the time you get your puppy, you have either a 10- or an eight-week window (depending on the age you bring him home) remaining of his key socialization period. At the 16-week point most experts agree that dogs become less receptive to novel experiences and it may be harder and take longer to get him accustomed to new things.

IMMUNITY VS. SOCIALIZATION

What should you do when you've also been told that your new puppy shouldn't socialize until he's had his final vaccination, which may not be until he's 16 weeks old? Is it safe to take him out and about before he's had his last puppy shot?

Socialization is so important that the answer may be yes. If you can arrange for your puppy to have his first vaccination early, at six weeks, he'll be afforded a degree of protection as the immunity he inherited from his mother fades out. And an under-socialized puppy who is fearful of new things because he wasn't exposed to them at the right time in his development runs risks equal to those of his catching something because his immunity isn't fully developed. However, try to avoid major dog-meeting places such as parks where all dog walkers congregate – as it's likely that some of those dogs won't be vaccinated. Instead look at quieter walks, where your puppy can experience new things in small increments – from experiencing different smells and textures under his feet to seeing such novelties as cyclists or swans. 'Socialization' doesn't mean taking your puppy everywhere, regardless of how crowded or noisy. Start small – an adventure for an eight-week-old puppy might be as simple as a trip down the street, a visit to a café, or an arranged meeting with a vaccinated, known-to-you, calm, older dog.

TOWN DOG/COUNTRY DOG

A puppy raised in town will quickly get used to traffic noise and the clanging and banging on city streets – but may startle badly at his first sight of a horse, while a country puppy may be relaxed around horses and cows, but terrified by the revving of a van nearby. Try to give your puppy the opportunity to accustom himself to sights and sounds outside his direct home environment.

▼ Playing safe
Ensure that any dogs your puppy meets before he's finished his vaccinations are up-to-date with their own shots, so that they're safe for him to have fun with.

EXPERIENCES CHECKLIST

Here are some of the things that your puppy should experience in the outside world in the weeks following his arrival with you. Aim to give him one or two new experiences a day, even if they are tiny ones. The following are examples; the list isn't comprehensive. Add anything you can think of, provided that it's controllable (by you) and not too extreme, noisy or shocking (for him).

Textures and surfaces

Accustom your puppy to different things under his paws:

- Grass
- Leaves
- Concrete
- Metal – such as street gratings and grilles (most vets' tables are metal)
- Water – puddles or deeper water if there's a shallow stream he can paddle in
- Carpet
- Tile and laminate.

Don't forget weather: take your puppy out whatever the weather; in rain, wind, sun or frost, even if only for very short times.

Other species

Start introductions at a distance, and in terms of cats, only introduce confident ones that won't run. Puppies usually develop a healthy respect for cats after one or two hisses and paw bats.

- Cat
- Horse
- Sheep
- Small mammals.

Other dogs

- Other puppies – many vets hold puppy parties, which are group meetings for puppies of the same age to meet and play, so take advantage of these.
- Calm, older dogs – ask around to find adult dogs who will put up with a rambunctious puppy and are up-to-date with their own vaccinations.

Objects

Where possible, give your puppy a chance to look closely at any or all of the following before he sees them 'in action' – so that he can deal with the appearance of the unfamiliar object before you add in the noise of it being in use:

- Ladder
- Bicycle
- Vacuum cleaner
- Skateboard
- Hairdryer.

When he's used to how they look, let him see/hear them in action, but at a distance, before gradually building to getting up close.

MEETING NEW
PEOPLE

We've looked at introducing your puppy to all kinds of new things, to other animals and to objects – but what about people? He needs to learn to expect the best from new people and to greet them happily and calmly.

GOING GENTLY

Patience will pay off when it comes to introducing your puppy to new people, particularly if he has a natural tendency to be shy. Make sure that he's allowed to approach new people in his own time, and let him retreat to the familiar when he needs to.

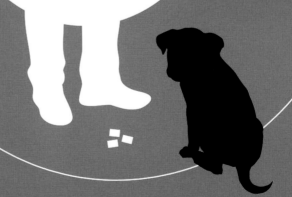

NEW PEOPLE

Don't overload him. The best way for a brand-new puppy to meet people at home is for them to pay him very little attention until he approaches them, and only then for them to make a fuss of him. If he's at the shy end of the spectrum, ask visitors to scatter treats around the floor, at a little distance from their feet. When he approaches closely enough to start scarfing up treats, ask a visitor to hold a treat out on a flat palm, and wait for the puppy to take it. If he isn't pushed towards people he's not yet certain of, he will make friends more quickly.

KEY RULES FOR CHILDREN'S BEHAVIOUR AROUND A PUPPY

Even small children should be taught the following rules:

- Puppies aren't toys and you shouldn't grab or pull at them.
- Don't wave your hands around a puppy's head – you'll scare him (show children how to stroke a puppy gently under the chin, so that he can see their hands).
- Don't run around or scream and shout around the puppy: any play should be quiet (teach children how to offer a puppy a treat, on the flat of the hand, to show him they're friendly).
- Don't disturb the puppy when he's resting or eating: leave him alone, and keep your distance.
- Don't take a puppy's toys unless you're in a supervised game together. You don't like people taking your things, so don't take his.

PEOPLE WITH REMOVABLE PARTS

As you'll see on pages 74-75, dogs don't understand that parts of people are removable. They regard the wheelchair, the stick, the hat and the furry-hooded parka as part of the picture they're looking at, not something separate from a person. Try to make sure he sees and becomes familiar with all kinds of people – young, old, tall, short, fast, slow – over his first few weeks with you, and let him see the 'props' (hats, coats, sticks) separately from the person, by laying them down at a distance and letting him examine them when he's ready.

SPECIAL MEASURES

Real care should be taken when introducing puppies to children, and they should never be left together unsupervised, even when they're playing happily. Teach children the five key rules of behaviour around a puppy (see box) to ensure that they do not tease or mishandle him without meaning to.

FIRST
VET VISIT

It's a good idea to make a first visit to the vet when your puppy doesn't actually need to have any procedures. Increasingly, vets offer 'pop-in' initial visits, in which your new puppy is introduced to the practice receptionist, is registered as a 'patient', gets to sniff around the waiting room, and may be popped on the vet table and gently handled, all accompanied by plenty of petting and treats. This is a great idea, particularly if your puppy is at the timid end of the scale – when he does need to have exams and shots, he'll be going into a situation where he's already had an enjoyable experience, so provided he's treated gently, he won't develop that dread of the vet that can make visits such a miserable experience with an adult dog.

BUILDING CONFIDENCE

Two or three decades ago, a puppy would simply have been expected to submit to handling from a stranger; how he felt about it would have been thought to be beside the point. But it's become clear that experiences in puppyhood carry forwards when dogs grow up, in particular during the key socialization period between the ages of four and 16 weeks. It's therefore especially important to ensure that puppies have as many positive experiences of life as possible, particularly social interaction with both dogs and people, during this 12-week window. Going slowly and gently with a young dog is no longer seen as 'spoiling' him; rather, it's perceived as an investment in creating a confident and stable adult dog.

◄ Positive vet vibes

When your puppy grows up, it's going to be much easier getting through the inevitable vet visits if he started off with positive associations. Make sure the first visit to the surgery is enjoyable (some vets actually hold puppy parties at their surgery to help).

WORMS AND FLEAS

Not a favourite topic, but if you're visiting the vet anyway, ask about worming. All puppies have worms (they are passed through the placenta from their mother), and your puppy should have been wormed as a matter of course at two, four and six weeks before he came to you. The vet will probably suggest an eight-week wormer, then one monthly until he is six months old. Opinions on the best frequency do vary a little, though, so take the advice given. Ask about flea prevention too.

◀ Itchy scratchy

If your puppy's scratching a lot, the cause may be fleas or other parasites. Medication (including flea collars) isn't usually recommended for very small puppies, so check with your vet what's safe to use when, and don't leave it too long: bad infestations of either can have an overall effect on your puppy's health.

DOG'S-EYE VIEW

HANDLE ME WITH CARE

I don't like it when people pick me up without warning, or touch my paws or my ears, although sometimes when I'm sleepy and sitting on a lap or the couch, it's comfortable to have my humans cuddle me and I don't mind it at all. Sometimes they brush me gently; they call it grooming and I enjoy that. If someone familiar takes liberties, I know that they're not going to hurt me, or allow anything bad to happen to me, because they've always protected me from things I'm scared of. When they introduce me to someone new, and that someone lets me sniff their hand and acts respectfully around me, I don't feel I have to protect myself; my humans have let me know it's going to be OK.

LEARNING TO
PLAY

Like many other juveniles, puppies are hardwired to play (they're engaging with their littermates and enjoying rough and tumble by the time they're four weeks old), and with a bit of planning, you can use play as a teaching tool, as well as an extra way to have fun and to bond with your new pet. Make sure that you reward 'good' play and discourage some of the less positive aspects. Left to themselves, puppies correct one another if play gets too nippy or rough, and over-enthusiastic puppies learn to tone it down – the reward is that the game continues, whereas the 'punishment' for a bitey puppy is that the play stops. Don't just play with your puppy, be his 'play policeman' too.

PUPPY/PERSON PLAY: GOOD GAMES, BAD GAMES

Play behaviours that might seem fun with a puppy can become a real pain with a full-sized adult dog. A tiny puppy scrabbling at your ankles for attention looks sweet, but when he's a year old, has tripled in size and reaches your waist when he jumps up, it's a nuisance. And it's not reasonable to expect your puppy to realize that he's suddenly become a play pest. So play fair with him, and don't laugh at or encourage behaviours that you won't like when he's older.

▶ **Play police**
Games work when you're both having fun, and play is an invaluable way to bond with your puppy. If he tips over and gets nippy or hysterically overexcited, have a few seconds out – it won't take long – to give him the chance to calm down.

PUPPY PROBLEMS

SETTING UP GOOD HABITS

Do

- Keep your hands gentle when you're playing with your puppy – however excitable he gets, don't bat or slap at him, even in fun. Many adult dogs love playing rough between themselves, but it's best to keep his dog-to-person play style 'soft'.

- Call a halt if he gets overexcited. Small puppies can tip into mad overexcitement very quickly. Just freeze, and stop play for 10 seconds or so – that's usually long enough to ramp things down a little.

- Play chase games – but always make sure he's chasing you, not the other way around. By the time he's a grown-up, you'll never be fast enough to catch him, so turning chasing him into a fun game can seriously damage his recall.

Don't

- Carry on playing if he nips. Simply make a yelping noise (this is what another puppy would do in dog-dog play), then turn away, bringing the game to a halt. Walk away if he tries to go on. This should stop a nipping habit developing.

- Hold him down for more than a second or two. While it's fine to restrain a puppy very gently, if he can't get away when he's really trying, he may feel trapped, and become frightened of playing – or overly defensive and nippy.

- Overdo it. The whole family may be happy to play with a cute puppy for hours, but he needs quiet time too, when he's not the focus of human attention. So play with him every day, but keep the sessions fairly short and don't try to continue play when he's settling down or already resting.

◀ **Tricks and games**
As he gets older, you can teach him tricks that will convert some bad habits into requested behaviour. For example, a puppy who likes to jump up can be taught that standing on his hind legs – when he's asked – can win him a treat.

WHAT KIND OF PLAY?

Play combines social interaction with physical exercise – it ticks all the boxes for a puppy. But it's also through play that you get glimpses of the sort of dog your puppy may grow up to be: assertive, timid, happy-go-lucky or intense. Just as you may have tested the way in which very small puppies reacted to being lightly restrained to see how amenable they might be to 'management' when you were viewing the new litter, so you can use play to get insights into the kind of canine personality your puppy will have when he's older.

HOW TO HELP WITH
CHEWING

By the time your puppy arrives with you at eight weeks plus, he will already be an enthusiastic chewer.

BE PREPARED

Your puppy's first set of teeth – small but sharp – will have begun to come through at between two and three weeks, and at that point his mother, unsurprisingly, will have begun weaning him. He'll keep his 28 'milk' teeth until the adult set start to come through when he's around four months old – and if you thought he was already keen on chewing before that, his second teething will break all previous records. Deal with that when you come to it, though – for now, puppy chewing is all you need worry about.

HOW HE CHEWS

Apart from needing to chew to relieve the discomfort of teething, your puppy also has a number of dedicated muscles which make chewing a deeply satisfying activity for him. Dogs don't chew food that's in small enough pieces to gulp down; for today's pets, chewing is really more like a well-loved hobby.

MASSETER

The masseter muscle is located in your puppy's cheek and is the main 'biting down' muscle used in chewing. It's extremely powerful: its development is one of the reasons that a mature dog's bite is so strong.

TEMPORALIS

The temporalis muscle is the largest in a dog's head. It lifts his jaw and works in a grinding action when he's chewing – if you look just behind and to the side of your puppy's head when he's eating a bone, you'll see it in action.

DIGASTRICUS

The digastricus muscle's job is primarily to open the jaw, running alongside and under the masseter, and extending beyond it. It works to help your puppy 'chow down' when he's chewing.

Puppies can chew most of the same things that adult dogs can, sometimes scaled down a little, although the very toughest types of chew (stag antlers, for example) may be best avoided until he's a little older. If he has plenty of available options when it comes to appropriate chews and chew toys, he's less likely to redirect his urge to chew onto things you'd prefer he didn't have – and the more accustomed he is to chewing familiar 'toys', the more readily he will turn to them during the teething stage when his adult teeth come through and make him uncomfortable.

CHEWING OPTIONS

Any or all of these will be appropriate for even a young puppy. Experiment to find his favourites.

▲ Rope toys

Go for sturdy twisted rope that will last and won't break into individual strands your puppy could swallow.

▲ Rawhide chews

Available in all sizes from tiny to gargantuan. Start smallish; too much rawhide in one go may cause a stomach upset.

▲ Kong toy

Hard rubber; slightly softer 'puppy' Kongs are available. Some shapes also act as treat toys: they can be filled with small biscuits or have meat paste or peanut butter smeared inside.

▲ Raw bones (never cooked)

Choose smaller sizes, or bones-and-meat combinations, such as a raw chicken wing. Many puppies will love a marrow bone, but the marrow is very rich, so scrape most of it out to avoid overload.

HOW TO HELP WITH CHEWING

UNDERSTANDING
'DISCIPLINE'

'Discipline' is in inverted commas in the title because small puppies don't really need disciplining; they need understanding and a tolerant approach to teaching them about life. The world is full of experts, though, and at some point you are bound to run into one or more when you're out with your puppy. You will probably get some unsolicited advice too.

THE BAGGAGE OF 'DOMINANCE'

If you're having a tricky time teaching your puppy to pee outside, or he's recently managed to find and destroy a favourite pair of shoes, you may be tempted to listen to the 'you're the boss' theory. But don't. While views on the best way to raise a puppy have changed a lot over time, there are still plenty of outdated myths doing the rounds, and many of them involve discipline and, above all, dominance.

The reason, you may be told, that you need to teach your puppy that you're the boss, is that if you don't, he will start to believe that *he* is the boss – and that can lead to problems. He will want to dominate you, and he will do this because, at heart, your cute puppy is a wolf. And wolves have a pack mentality: every one of them wants to be a pack leader.

DOG'S-EYE VIEW

GETTING WHAT I WANT

I belong to one of the most cooperative species on Earth. Dogs are social, and we've learned how to get what we want by cooperating both with people and with each other. I don't want to run your life, much less dominate you: I want to have a good time, with regular food, exercise and company, and it seems to me that the surest way to get these things is to watch you, the controller of most of the good stuff in my life, carefully. I see what sorts of behaviour get me which benefits, and my strategy pays off: it's socially savvy. I'm smart, not 'dominant'.

The myth and the language of dominance persisted for a long time and made quite a few dogs' lives difficult. All kinds of behaviour, from sitting on the couch to walking through doors ahead of their humans, were attributed to dogs wanting to be dominant, and all sorts of techniques were developed to change their minds – from 'alpha rolls', in which owners were taught to force their pets onto the floor and stand over them, to feeding dogs only after their people had eaten.

Eventually, though, the ideas began to be debunked. Wolves, researchers found, actually made their packs work through highly cooperative behaviour, and rarely fought amongst themselves. Dogs, moreover, aren't wolves: they have lived with humans for thousands of generations, and they are very good at it.

It's true that you are 'management' to your dog. You control his resources: food, walks and social interaction. You're his company and he lives in your house; you don't live in his. Your puppy may look at ways he can get more of the good stuff by using any method that works, from the rightly named 'puppy eyes' to seeing if he can get into the cupboard where the treats are kept. As a benign manager, you can work on a swap system: he does what you want (sits quietly in the car) and you do what he wants (open the door to let him out for his walk). That's what cooperation is, and it can work very well. So if people start to describe more disciplinarian 'domination'-based ways of management, don't listen. They're out of date.

▼ **Give and take**
In the to-and-fro of play that you're both enjoying, puppies may actually self-handicap – that is, play at less than their maximum strength – in order to prolong the game.

CHAPTER TWO

SETTLING **IN**

The previous chapter gave you and your puppy quite a packed schedule to follow, and filled in some of the thinking behind the basics – what he eats, where he sleeps and so on. This section looks at the overall developmental progress you can expect him to make over the next few weeks and months, and at how you can begin to manage some common puppy stages – helping him overcome fear, for example, or teaching him to spend some time on his own without fretting. It also shows you how to make a start on some very simple training with your puppy: 'Sit', 'Down', and walking on a lead.

IN THE FIRST WEEK:
COLLARS & TEETH

He's been home for a few days, he's met his immediate household, and he's starting to know when he can expect his meals and where he's expected to settle down at bedtime. Here are two things to fit in after a few days:

WEARING A COLLAR

If you haven't already done it, put his collar on. Although he won't be out and about much for some weeks yet, get him used to wearing a collar before it's a necessity. The collar should be narrow, fabric, with a flat buckle or slot-in clasp, and loose enough to be comfortable. With older puppies and dogs, you should be able easily to slip two fingers into the space between collar and neck; with a smaller puppy, if you can slip one finger between collar and neck, that's loose enough. Most puppies squirm a bit at the unfamiliar feeling when they first wear a collar (and a very few really dislike it) but if you leave it on and distract him with a game or a toy, he'll forget he's wearing it within a day or two. When he's used to the collar, add the tag. Take it off last thing at night if he's more comfortable sleeping without it. Puppies grow at a phenomenal rate, so check how tight his collar is regularly and replace it as soon as he's outgrown it.

▶ **Lead or harness?**
For a frisky puppy, a harness may be an easier and more comfortable option for walking than a lead attached to a collar (it's not instead of a collar, which he should be wearing anyway). It guides his whole body, takes the pressure off his neck and can also help to avoid excessive pulling.

TOOTHBRUSHING

Most owners still don't brush their dogs' teeth. Which is a pity, because dental problems in older dogs account for a huge amount in vets' bills every year, and regular brushing can be helpful in avoiding them. It really is worth it.

If you get your dog used to it when he's still a puppy, it takes no longer and is no trickier than brushing your own teeth – but it must be done every day to be effective. It's important *never* to use human toothpaste, as it contains xylitol, which is poisonous to dogs. Buy dog toothpaste, which is usually meat-flavoured and so likely to be popular with your puppy. You can use a small toothbrush that you fit on a fingertip.

HOW TO DO IT

Spend a few days getting him used to the idea of toothbrushing.
- The first time, wipe a tiny taste of toothpaste onto his front teeth.
- The following day, wipe around his mouth (gently) with a tiny bit of toothpaste on a clean fingertip.
- The next day, gently 'brush' his front teeth only, using the toothpaste and the fingertip brush.

And so on, building up gradually until you are using the brush to go all round the inside and outside of both his upper and lower teeth.

Don't grab him or frighten him; if he starts to look apprehensive when the toothpaste comes out, take a step or two back in the process – just wiping a tiny taste of toothpaste on his front teeth again – until he's comfortable with the idea.

▲ **Tooth care**
It's worth caring for your dog's teeth assiduously, because dental work for dogs, just as for humans, can be prohibitively expensive. Most puppies, once they're used to the idea, don't mind having their teeth brushed.

DOG'S-EYE VIEW

TOUCH AND TRUST

I let you handle me because I trust you. Back when I was with my canine family our parents played with us gently, even when we nipped, but every so often we'd get a low growl to give us a warning that we were being rude and taking the play-biting too far. My mother was never rough with us, though, and I know that you'd never restrain me by force either. On the whole I stay still because you ask me to, not because I think you'll make me if I don't.

HOW LONG
WILL IT TAKE?

Puppies vary a good deal in the speed at which they learn, and they grow up at slightly different rates. It's usually said that smaller breeds mature faster than large ones, and while it's true that giant breeds can take anything up to three years to mature completely, even small dogs can't really be considered fully mature until they're around two years old.

CHECKLIST FOR YOU

And you're just at the start of the journey, so if you find yourself wondering 'how long will it take?' (for him to become house-trained, to play without nipping, to understand that a game's over…), do a mental check to see if you're playing your part by teaching him as well as you can. Following a few guidelines can make a big difference.

- Are you completely consistent in your dealings with your puppy?
- Is everyone else around him consistent?
- Are you making time to spend one-to-one with him, mixing playing and training, every day?
- Does the whole household know the routine for his house-training, and are there people keeping an eye on the schedule so that he gets out frequently, ideally *before* he needs to pee?
- Is he getting enough downtime? Is he being left alone to rest when he naps during the day?

▼ Larger breeds
Bigger breeds can seem much slower to grow up than their littler contemporaries. A Jack Russell terrier, for example, may be quite mature at 9 months old, while a Labrador or an Old English sheepdog may not seem really grown up until they reach 18 months or so.

BE CONSISTENT

Puppies will learn faster if they trust you and if they can rely on you to be predictable. Provided that he's kindly treated, a puppy will accept the circumstances you decide for him – whether your dog sleeps on your bed or in his crate, for example, is up to you, and he'll settle for either, but don't be changeable and suddenly

50

DOG'S-EYE VIEW

CONSISTENCY MATTERS

I watch you carefully to see if I can understand
what you mean – don't forget, I only have
body language, not speech, to work with – but
sometimes, however hard I try, you muddle
me. Remember, if you want me to repeat a
behaviour, you have to send me the same signals
as the last time; if you don't, I won't get it, and
we'll both get frustrated. Consistency matters:
sometimes, when you think I'm being 'naughty',
I'm actually confused.

decide that, having slept on the bed, he's now to be relegated to
the crate because he's getting too big and too old. Decide what
boundaries you're going to set early on and stick with them.
He'll find that much easier to deal with than alternate bouts of
indulgence and strictness.

PUT YOURSELF IN HIS PAWS

There's an exercise that some dog behaviourists practise when
they're teaching people how to communicate with their dogs,
which is to pair up owners (no dogs allowed) and give them simple
messages to convey to each other. But they're not allowed to
speak. The resulting frustrations bring it home to them what it's
like to be a dog trying to understand what a none-too-skilled
owner is trying to convey.

Try a variation of it with your puppy: see if you can engage him in
an activity without using words at all. He won't have a problem:
after all, he spends most of his time reading your body language
rather than listening to your words. But you may find it nearly
impossible even to play a game with him without keeping up a
running commentary. You'll find it a (possibly humbling) reminder
that, far from being slow, our dogs are outstandingly skilled at
picking up the, often muddled, signals we send.

▲ **Keeping it basic**
Make it worth his while to obey
you. Seeing a positive for him in
something that you want him to
do – at its most basic, paw for a
treat – will always work better
than 'Do it because I say so.'

DEVELOPMENT
MILESTONES

Birth–2 weeks
- He can feel and smell, but not yet see or hear (his eyes will open after he's about 10 days old, and his ear canals at about two weeks). He can't warm his own body, or eliminate his own waste: he relies on his mother for everything; she not only feeds but washes her puppies constantly.
- His cry is surprisingly loud and piercing if he's cold or hungry.
- He spends around 10 per cent of his time feeding, the other 90 per cent, asleep.

2–3 weeks
- His hearing and sight begin to develop, but aren't strong yet.
- He is starting to stand and walk.
- Most puppies can bark and wag their tails by the third week.

3–4 weeks
- As he moves around more, he starts to interact with his littermates. At four weeks, most puppies have started to play.
- His sight and hearing have become more acute.
- His baby teeth begin to come through – incisors first, followed by canines, and finally molars.
- His mother will begin to wean him as her milk supply starts to dry up. By four weeks he will be ready to try out solid food.

4 weeks
- The key socialization stage – the time at which puppies willingly accept and build on new experiences – begins around now, and continues until about 16 weeks old.

A lot is now known about the different stages a puppy goes through as he matures. These pages offer you an overview of how a puppy develops from birth through to adolescence, and shows you what's happening in his mind (even as you marvel at how he's finally growing into his paws).

5–7 weeks

- He's becoming bolder and more adventurous in exploring and playing with his siblings.
- He's beginning to learn to inhibit his bite to prolong play.
- He's developing the beginnings of bladder and bowel control, and will try to move away from his sleeping spot to eliminate.
- Weaning continues and should be complete by the end of week seven.

8–10 weeks

- At eight weeks old, he'll have a complete set of 28 milk or puppy teeth.
- By nine weeks, his senses are fully developed.
- Between eight and 10 weeks, he may exhibit a phenomenon known, rather bleakly, as the first fear imprint period – as the name suggests, this shows up as an exaggerated caution and fear of new things. Careful socialization is particularly important if he's showing fear: he needs to be exposed to plenty of new things, but in a positive and unintimidating way. This coincides with the time at which naturally he'd be exploring outside the 'den' on his own, so probably originally evolved to teach him caution in new surroundings.

10–12 weeks

- From 10 weeks, most puppies play and explore for most of the time they're awake.
- At 12 weeks, his adult teeth start to come through in earnest and he needs to spend a lot of time chewing to relieve the pain in his gums.
- He will have his final vaccination at 12 weeks. Some vets recommend you wait a week after this final shot to be on the safe side, but after that he can safely go anywhere.

DEVELOPMENT
MILESTONES

13–16 weeks

- By 13 weeks, your puppy is beginning to be a teenager and, just like his human equivalent, his behaviour may become more testing. He may appear to forget things he mastered weeks before, and he may challenge the status quo.

16 weeks to 6 months

- By the time he's about six months old, all 48 of his adult teeth will have come through.
- At six months plus, male puppies start to leg-lift when they pee, and bitches may come into heat as early as five months. Growing sexual maturity means that hormones go through the roof ('teenage' males have more than five times as much testosterone coursing through their systems as adult males, and dogs may begin adult-style posturing.

6 months onwards

- Some behaviourists identify the time between six and 14 months as the second fear imprint period, during which puppies are cautious about new situations and may suddenly exhibit fear around things which, to the human eye, are completely unthreatening.

WHAT HIS PEOPLE CAN DO

3 weeks
- His interests are growing beyond food and warmth; he can be gently handled and socialized with people.

6–8 weeks
- He'll go to his new home.
- From six weeks, he's old enough for short sessions of training – and training and reinforcement should go on for the rest of his lifetime.
- House-training can begin.

8–10 weeks
- He may react with fear to random unfamiliar things, and needs to be carefully desensitized to stop the fear becoming 'set'.
- He will be starting to learn to walk on the lead.
- His humans should try to 'vet' the other dogs he meets and ensure they're stable and calm. To meet and socialize with other puppies, he could attend 'puppy parties' organized by the vet's surgery. Socializing with different dogs of different ages will help him become fluent with dogs generally.

6–16 weeks
- Socialization, socialization, socialization... He should be introduced to as wide a variety of situations, people, animals and objects as his owners can manage.

8 weeks–6 months
- He needs to chew constantly, so should be offered a range of suitable things, from rawhide and rubber toys to natural (raw) bones.

13 weeks
- House rules may need tightening up as your puppy becomes a teenager.

4 months
- Owners need to decide about neutering or spaying their puppy. Take veterinary advice to make the decision.
- From four months to one year, a puppy's growth spurt means that a careful eye needs to be kept on his diet, to make sure he's getting enough calories to support his growth (most puppies will have reached their adult height by a year, but may still have a lot of filling out to do).

TEACHING
'WATCH ME'

Most small puppies will find you, their human, one of the most fascinating things imaginable. As your puppy gets older you'll find that his attention is pulled all over the place, so while he's still young (and you're still so interesting), teach him to pay attention to you whenever he's asked. This is one of the first and the most valuable things you'll teach him – that looking to you brings dividends.

HOW TO DO IT

'Watch me' is simple to teach. Every time your puppy looks at you, he gets a treat. You aren't allowed to try to attract his attention, though – he has to look voluntarily. And, as usual when you're teaching him something, the treats, though tiny, should be high-value, not just ordinary pieces of kibble or biscuit.

Start outdoors, in the garden, where there's plenty of interest, but nothing terribly distracting. Put your puppy on a loose lead, so he's standing near you, rather than wandering off, but don't direct him otherwise. Don't do anything to attract his attention, and certainly don't show him the treats (keep them accessible, though).

Keep an eye on him, but not too obviously – that is, don't stand staring at him. The moment he turns to look at you, though – *of his own volition* – fish out a treat and give it to him. Go back to what you were doing, even if that was just contemplating garden jobs that need doing.

◄ **Getting his attention**
Treating your dog when he looks at you – even if it's involuntary – is a great way to reinforce the idea that you're an all-round 'good thing', and that it's worth paying attention.

Carry on keeping an eye on him, covertly. When he looks at you again, treat him. Don't extend the contact into a game or a longer interaction – just keep treating him when he looks at you. After around 10 treats, move on to something else – you can start to practise 'Sit' or 'Down', or go back to your own everyday activities.

HOW TO BUILD ON IT

Practise every day, treating him whenever he looks at you, but gradually taking him to increasingly distracting locations. The more there is to look at, the better he's doing when he chooses to look at you. When he's familiar with the pattern – look at you, get a treat – add a verbal cue – 'Watch me' – just before he gets the treat. Use it consistently and keep up the practice every few days even when he's completely familiar with the sequence.

▼ Look, treat

At first, you're going to be using quite a lot of treats, so make sure they're something fairly healthy and very small. At he gets used to the routine, you'll gradually be able to phase the treats out; eventually 'Watch me!' will get his attention automatically.

DOG'S-EYE VIEW

MY KEY FOCUS

You were already interesting, but you've started a new game: every time I even look at you, I get a treat and a 'Good boy!', so you've become more attractive than ever. I'm learning that paying attention to you pays off. It helps to know this, because it means that in tricky situations, I can look to you for help in understanding what's going on (and how you're expecting me to behave).

▶ Play to win

Go slowly, and start when there isn't too much going on. He needs to learn it first when he isn't already going full pelt with another absorbing activity or game.

TEACHING 'WATCH ME'

TEACHING
'SIT' & 'DOWN'

Humans tend to think of 'training' as belonging in a different compartment from playing or just going about everyday activities with a puppy tagging alongside. But in a puppy's mind there isn't any difference: he's keen to have as much contact and interaction as he can with you, and a couple of minutes' training, whether it's learning to sit or walking on a lead, can be mixed in with anything else that's going on in his day.

This more inclusive way of thinking about it means that you can fit in a bit of training whenever you have a few spare minutes and you're in the mood. And you can start as soon as you bring your puppy home, provided that you keep sessions fun and very short. Think in terms of two or three minutes – which is about as long as you can expect your new puppy's attention span to last).

'SIT'
When your puppy is standing in front of you, take a treat and lift it up and back, over his head and between his ears (don't lift it up high, or he'll jump to reach it instead of sitting). As he lifts his head to follow it, his rear end will automatically go down and hit the floor. Give him the treat and repeat the process. When you've been practising for a few days, you can add the cue 'Sit' as you

take the treat up over his head. Once he's made the association between word and action, you can gradually remove the lure, and simply ask him to 'Sit', then treat him when he does.

KEEP IT VARIED

Practise 'Sit' and 'Down' a few times in different situations every day. You don't need to set up a 'formal' practice – in fact, it's better if, once he's mastered the basics, you don't; just ask for them in passing – a sit while you're playing with him, for instance, or a down while you're preparing his dinner.

SAY IT WITH BODY LANGUAGE

I understand a bit of what you say, but it's still easier for me to look at what you're saying with your body – that's just what dogs do, both with each other and with their people. You don't seem to be naturally as good at reading body language as I am: perhaps that's why you need words to back it up.

'DOWN'

To teach 'Down', you can lure your puppy down to the floor from a sit. While he's still sitting, take another treat, hold it level with your puppy's nose, then bring it down to floor level. If you pull it forwards, he'll probably get up from his sit – keep it level with your puppy's nose, so that he'll follow it down, and his legs will slide forwards until he's lying down. It's not quite such a natural, easy posture as a sit, so give it two or three goes per session until he gets the idea. As soon as he's in a lying position, hand over the treat. As with 'Sit', only add the verbal cue, 'Down', when he clearly understands what the lure down to the floor means, and he's lying down every time. That way, you're labelling a behaviour that he's already learned rather than adding words when he's not yet quite sure what he's supposed to do.

COMING
BACK

When you can call your puppy in the absolute confidence that he'll come back to you, you've taught him one of the most useful things he will ever learn. The more certain you are of his recall, the more freedom you'll be able to give him, and the earlier you start to teach him, the more habitual his return to you will be. So begin with the chase game when he's very small – within a day or two of his arriving home with you.

This is the very first step in teaching recall. Getting a puppy to chase after you should be easy; he's hardwired to want to be part of the gang, and he loves running around. All you have to do is make yourself the most attractive thing to run after. You can start the chase game anywhere where's there's space to take a few turns – out in the garden, or even in the house if there's enough room.

1

Keep it up for a minute or two, turning in different directions, letting him almost catch up with you, then running away again, before letting him finally catch you, rewarding him with the toy or treat, and making a big fuss of him. Play the same game every day, and ensure that there's always a positive payoff when your puppy 'catches' you.

2

Start by engaging with him, get down to his level, make a fuss of him, perhaps let him see a toy or treat you're holding. Then stand up and run away from him. You can clap your hands or call 'Come!' or make whooping noises as you run, pause to let him catch up with you, then take off again. Don't worry about looking silly; to your puppy you'll be the most entertaining thing in his day.

WHO'S CHASING WHO?

Make sure you get it the right way around: your puppy should be chasing you, rather than you haring after him.

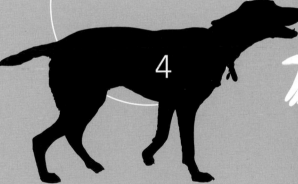

When you feel that chasing you has become a habit, begin stopping more frequently and encourage him to come to you when you're not moving. Crouch down, pat your leg and call 'Come!' When he reaches you, treat him. At this stage, begin to touch his collar before giving him another treat. In the future, when you call him to you, it will often be to put his lead on, and the earlier that you make holding his collar part of the sequence, the more accepting he will be of it when you actually need to.

3

4

As your puppy grows bigger and more aware of his surroundings, it will become more of a challenge for you to remain at the centre of his focus. Keep up the interest by starting a game, and then running away as you're still playing, and as soon as he catches up with you, reward him by taking up the game where you left off. Make the exercise part of your regular play with him, and use the 'Come' cue whenever you're at the point of calling him over to you.

61

COMING BACK

ONCE MORE – WITH DISTRACTIONS

When you know that your puppy will run the length of the garden to you when you call him – every time you call him – take him somewhere where there is more in his surroundings to distract him. Set him up to succeed, though – don't take him straight from the garden to a park where all the local dog walkers congregate. Try a quiet corner of a local recreation ground, or somewhere similar, and clip a long line to his collar to avoid any problems if unexpected distractions turn up.

Let him have a brief wander and sniff, so that he's aware of more potential spots of interest than he would have in your garden, but keep it short. Then call him from slightly further away than he's used to. Have a treat bonus ready for him when he comes – the transition from home turf to outside is a big enough deal for you to bring out the liver cake or chicken pieces or whatever favourite will act as the biggest motivator. When he comes, praise him, play with him a little, then repeat the exercise. Only take up the line after two or three successful recalls: you don't want him to think that coming back to you invariably means that he'll be taken away from whatever he was exploring.

What if he doesn't come? Don't call him more than a couple of times; if he doesn't come the second time, go up to him and gather up the long line, without appearing cross, either in word or body language, and walk him home. Then take things back a stage – practise a little more in the garden before trying again. The mistake you can make at this stage is to keep calling when he won't come back: if you do this, in effect you're teaching him to ignore you. If he learns, instead, that ignoring you means the loss of his roaming privileges, it will ultimately strengthen his recall rather than damaging it.

Take your time teaching him recall: it's so important that it's worth increasing both distance and distractions in tiny increments so that he's sure to learn. When – probably after a period of months, not weeks – you're confident that he'll come, you can get rid of the long line. And when he's playing with other dogs and you can call him away from across the park successfully, you'll know that you've done a great job.

SURPRISE GIFTS

One of the most effective things that you can use when you're teaching your puppy is the element of surprise. Many trainers recommend that every so often, rather than giving him a single treat when he does what you've asked, you offer a bonus – a handful of treats, all in one go. He'll be amazed by his good luck, and it will motivate him to come back the next time, just to see if it will happen again. Keep it a fairly rare event, though, so that he doesn't get blasé about the occasional windfall.

◄ Exploring safely
A long line is an invaluable aid when you're teaching your puppy to come back to you – he doesn't have the restriction of a lead, but there's something you can take hold of if you need to, to keep him safe (or if he has a blip, and simply refuses to come back!)

WALKING
ON A LEAD

With a little patience and perseverance, you can start to teach even a small puppy to walk on the lead, although be prepared for him to do plenty of wandering around you as he learns. It's not behaviour that comes naturally to dogs, who don't make a habit of strolling side by side as humans do, so accept that it will take a while, and keep the sessions short (for a 10-week-old puppy, say, five minutes is plenty).

STARTING OUT
You need a pocketful of tiny, high-value treats and a lead. It's best to practise in your garden or another enclosed place without many distractions. Clip the lead on your puppy's collar, but leave the other end trailing for the first session or two.

1 Start by letting your puppy know that you have treats. Take a step or two, then give your puppy the treat. Get out another and hold it in a closed hand down by your left leg. Walk another couple of steps, and give him the treat if he's still by your side.

2 Gently pick up the loose end of the lead and start to walk slowly, in a circle. Try to keep your puppy at your left side by holding a treat down by your leg and giving it to him every few paces provided he's still in place. If he wanders, pat your leg again, and give him the treat as soon as he's back in position.

Most people prefer their dog to walk on their left side, with the lead held in the right hand, so he needs to get used to being on your left. He'll stay by your side, anticipating the treat, so stand still and feed him another couple of treats while he's beside you. Spend a few minutes every day practising, but as he gets better at following you, phase out the treats so that they become occasional, rather than constant.

What do you do if, instead of walking alongside you, he starts to jump up to grab the treat? Say 'Uh-uh', and stop dead. Stand still until his feet are back on the ground, then start again from the beginning, patting your leg and encouraging him to follow the treat.

The advantage of starting this while he's so young is that you stand a good chance of having him walking nicely on a lead by the time his puppy adolescence kicks in. As he gets more used to following you, try some changes in pace – walking especially slowly, or running, with him following alongside – and practise in busier places, walking along roads or through shopping streets. The aim is to get him to stick by you, no matter what else is going on. When he's walking reliably next to you, add a verbal cue to start him off, or recall him back to position if he begins to wander – most people use 'Heel'.

3 It's easier to keep him with you if you start to pick up the pace and take fairly constant turns. That way, he has to keep up with where you are in order to get the next treat. Try to end each session at the point where you're walking together at a fairly brisk pace – even if that only lasts a moment or two. Finish by asking your puppy for a sit and give him a final treat.

▼ **Daily practice**
Little and often is the best way to get your puppy comfortably walking alongside you. Keep practice sessions to just a few minutes at a time while he gets used to the idea.

WALKING ON A LEAD

BAD GAMES,
GOOD GAMES

Playing games with a cooperative puppy is about as much fun you can have, but it's important to keep his manners up to scratch and make sure that he doesn't get into poor play habits. Dogs put up with all kinds of play offences in small puppies, but give them increasingly short shrift as they mature.

◄ Laughing along
Most puppies have a natural sense of mischief which can be very appealing, so it's important to decide where your personal boundaries for his behaviour are before he begins to decide that he can get away with too much because he makes you laugh.

FOUR PLAY HABITS TO BREAK

Most puppies probably do all four of these at one time or another. Some are fine for when he's playing with another dog, who isn't likely to complain about him jumping up or chasing, but not appropriate for person/puppy play. Nipping and barging aren't usually welcomed by anyone, whether person or dog. Here's how to stop them.

Nipping

All puppies nip when they're playing, but with teeth like needles (and that's just his first set), it's a habit to discourage. It's easy to stop, although it may take a few attempts. When you're playing, the moment his teeth snag your skin, make a loud 'Ow!' exclamation, get up, disengage and turn away. Don't make eye contact; turn your back and walk away. When you start to play again, if it happens again, repeat the process. Repeat whenever he brings his teeth out. Although you may find yourself bringing play to a halt often over the first day or two, he'll soon learn that teeth stop play.

Jumping up

This is natural behaviour in a puppy: young dogs like to reach and lick a parent's or older dog's face. Although it's actually a deferential sign, it's a pain when it becomes a habit. He wants to get to your face, so make it unrewarding by turning your body away from him as he jumps. Then (and this is one of those moves that calls for good timing), the second his feet are back on the floor, turn back to him, ask for a sit, and praise and pet him when he sits. He wants your attention, and when he realizes that jumping won't work, he'll stop.

One-way chase

Chase is many dogs' favourite game, and a pair of dogs will often reverse the parts midway through, so that the chaser becomes the chased and vice versa. But even a fast human doesn't have a chance of catching even a slow dog once he reaches six months or so and, given that the last thing you want him to do is run away from you and enjoy your failure to catch him, make sure the only way your puppy plays 'it' with you is by chasing after you. If he tries to entice you to chase him with play bows, turn and run away from him. Most dogs love chasing as much as they love being chased, so he'll take up the challenge.

▼ **Playing 'It'**
He'll soon be able to outrun you, so make sure that games of chase go in one direction only.

DOG'S-EYE VIEW

THE TOLERANCE ZONE

The grown-up dogs I lived with when I was tiny had a lot of patience with me and my siblings, even when we trampled all over them and nipped. I'm the only dog in my new home, but we do have grown-up dogs visiting and I've noticed that now I'm bigger (almost six months now), they don't put up with the same sort of behaviour. In fact, I've been growled at quite nastily when they thought I was being rude. I suppose they're teaching me manners along with my humans – at least, I do stop when they growl.

Barging

It's rude behaviour even between dogs, and barging into you, either as an attempted provocation to induce play, or simply to get past you where it matters (such as at the front door), can be both irritating and, in its livelier manifestations, as when he runs full-tilt and on purpose into the back of your legs, actively painful. The way to deal with it is to back him up and body-block him, good-temperedly but in a way that shows him you mean business. A body block is exactly how it sounds: you use your body to 'block' him and get him to back up. If he tries to go round you, you move forwards or to the side, so that you're blocking him off. When he's calmed down, step aside. Body-blocking is useful in any circumstances when you want to deny him access to something specific too.

BAD GAMES, GOOD GAMES

AT THE
DOOR

Good manners around the front door become more and more important as your puppy grows; a small puppy barking and jumping at visitors may look sweet, but a fully-grown dog doing the same thing can be a real nuisance, and, if he develops into a door-dasher, becomes a risk to himself as well as an annoyance to everyone else. If you start early, you can teach him to stand back before greeting people politely. Because the front door is generally an exciting place for him, it's a good idea to begin teaching him calm behaviour around it long before he reaches the (sometimes defiant) adolescent stage.

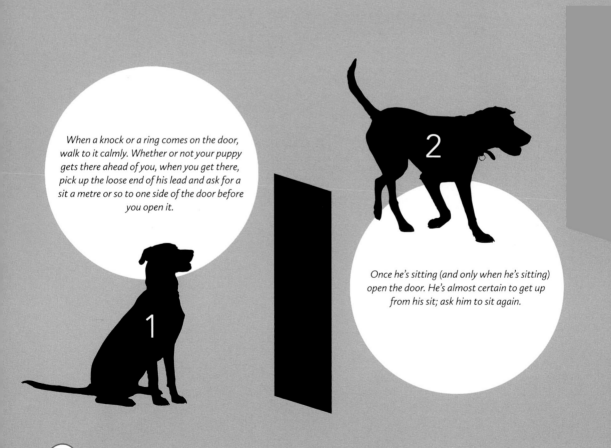

When a knock or a ring comes on the door, walk to it calmly. Whether or not your puppy gets there ahead of you, when you get there, pick up the loose end of his lead and ask for a sit a metre or so to one side of the door before you open it.

Once he's sitting (and only when he's sitting) open the door. He's almost certain to get up from his sit; ask him to sit again.

A short, lightweight lead clipped to his collar is helpful while you're teaching – you can leave the end trailing most of the time, but it means that you can lead him away from the door if he gets too excited. Let visitors know in advance what you want them to do (a bit of simple cooperative choreography is needed to make this work) and set up several 'visits' a day as you begin to teach him, even if the visitors are only members of the household walking outside the house to the front door. Leave a box of puppy treats outside the door so that they can collect one as they arrive.

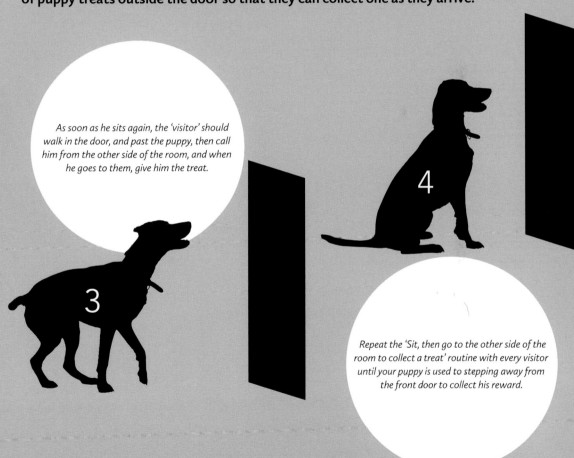

As soon as he sits again, the 'visitor' should walk in the door, and past the puppy, then call him from the other side of the room, and when he goes to them, give him the treat.

Repeat the 'Sit, then go to the other side of the room to collect a treat' routine with every visitor until your puppy is used to stepping away from the front door to collect his reward.

TIME
ALONE

Dogs like company; being alone isn't a natural state of affairs for them. But your puppy is inevitably going to have to spend some time on his own, and it's kinder and more effective to start to leave him for short periods sooner rather than later. Start soon after you get him, gently, when you're at home, and build up the time gradually, so that when, after plenty of practice, you do have to go out and leave him for a while, he's used to the routine.

WHEN AND WHERE?

Choose a time when he's been using up plenty of energy on a walk or playing, so that he's likely to take a rest shortly. Take him outside for a few minutes to ensure that he won't need a pee as soon as you leave him, then come in, take him to the room you've chosen and leave him quietly, shutting the door behind you. It's usually easiest to practise leaving him in the kitchen or utility room – it should have a solid door you can shut. His bed or crate should be in a corner.

HOW LONG?

He's almost certain to fuss – you'll hear crying and whining, and he may scrabble at the door. Ignore this and wait until silence falls. He may just stop fussing, or – since you took him in when he was tired already – he may have fallen asleep. Whichever is the case, open the

▼ **Home alone**
You shouldn't leave a very small puppy for more than an hour, at most. Try a few 'starter' sessions of just fifteen minutes or so, leaving him somewhere safe, with a comfortable bed or crate.

KEEPING ME CALM

I use my human's body language to tell how she feels about leaving me alone. I can tell she's not stressed about going out, and this makes me relax. I've noticed that she goes out without making a big deal about it, so it seems that it shouldn't be anything for me to worry about.

door only when he's stopped fussing. If he's a determined whiner, wait patiently for a moment of silence, and time it so you open the door just as soon as he's quiet. If you time your return while he's still crying, you're teaching him that making a fuss will bring you back. If you wait until he's quiet, you're reinforcing the quiet behaviour instead.

When you open the door, if he rushes out, don't make a fuss – just encourage him into the garden, in case he needs a wee, and carry on with your everyday activities. If he's fallen asleep, leave the door open; he'll come and find you when he wakes up. Ultimately, you want being left to seem like no big deal to your puppy – something that may not be particularly welcome, but that isn't a drama.

Even if you don't need to, make sure you leave your puppy for a little time every day. As he gets older, you can make the periods longer. By the time you're leaving him for half an hour plus, start to give him a chew toy as you leave, such as a Kong, stuffed with something special that will take a bit of time and effort to get out. If the filling is something he really loves, and he only gets it when he's going to be alone for a while, he can keep himself occupied while you're away.

IN THE LONG TERM...

Most experts believe that even an adult dog shouldn't be left alone for more than four hours at a time. You can build to this gradually, but don't try to get there too fast. Work up to leaving your puppy for up to an hour at three to four months, and between two and three hours when he's six to seven months old.

▲ **Killing time**
A filled Kong toy can be a popular way for your puppy to wile away time while you're out. Some sorts can be filled with tiny kibble that will take him some time to extract.

FRIGHTENED
PUPPY

What puppies are afraid of, and how afraid they are, varies hugely, just as it does with people. If you have a bold puppy, you may not see any evidence of fear, or even much caution for a while; if, on the other hand, he's shy, you may read signs that he's fearful around a whole variety of things.

Fear is a problem not only because it makes your puppy feel bad, but because it's at the root of the vast majority of behavioural problems – a scared dog may run away or become unpredictable or snappy if he feels he has to deal directly with something he perceives as a danger. It's your job to show him that you've got his back. Familiarize yourself with what puppy fear looks like, and look at ways to build his confidence gradually around the things that cause him to be afraid.

Research has shown that puppies are particularly susceptible to fear of the unfamiliar at specific times during their development – between eight and 10 weeks, and over a later, longer period between six and 14 months – so there are likely to be times when your puppy needs specific help to overcome specific fears.

▼ Feeling scared
Your puppy may be frightened by something that's quite obvious to you – a car backfiring, for example, or a crowd of people around him. At other times, it may not be quite so clear, and it will be left to you to work it out.

WHAT FEAR LOOKS LIKE – AND HOW TO DEAL WITH IT

Signs that your puppy is afraid include:

- Backing off
- Ears or head down, and back flat
- Eyes wide and rounded, particularly if the whites are showing
- Tail held down, or tucked between his legs
- Lots of tongue flicking or yawning.

IF HE'S FEARFUL

Do:

- Stay cool, and keep your voice calm and reassuring
- If possible, move the source of the fear further away
- If that's not possible, move the puppy further away
- Take it slowly. If he's already afraid, it's best to get him out of the situation, then make a plan to deal with the fear when the same situation arises again.

Don't:

- Laugh at him
- Move the frightening thing closer to him (if it's a person, ask them to back off)
- Move him forcibly closer to the frightening thing ('showing' him that there's nothing to be frightened of probably won't work)
- Make a big fuss, consoling and comforting him.

▶ **Dropped head, rounded back**
He's 'making himself small' – it's a characteristic posture in a scared pup.

▶ **Tongue flick with a paw lift**
An appealing look from a puppy who's puzzled and apprehensive. The tongue flick shows uncertainty; the paw lift is often an appeal to an owner.

▶ **Tucked tail**
A tail tucked under is always a worried or fearful signal, and while this puppy is facing forwards, his body is pulling back.

73

MANAGING
FEAR

Let's say that the thing that sent your puppy into a tailspin of fear was someone in a parka with a big, furry hood. Since dogs often don't understand clothes as things you take off or add, he may not even have realized that there was a person inside.

Going at your puppy's own pace may mean that progress is quite slow, but don't worry: if he's allowed to let go of his fear step by gradual step, not only are the effects more likely to be permanent, but his trust in you will grow.

Don't encourage him to 'man up' and face the fear, or hug him to you with noisy consolation: either will usually make things worse. Instead, look at ways to introduce the source of the fear – whether it's a kitchen blender at full blend, a vacuum cleaner, a passing cyclist, or a man in a hat – in a controlled way, at a distance, in very small quantities and with appealing reinforcements.

2

Having taken your puppy away from, for example, the scary-parka person who first frightened him, make sure that the next time he sees the parka, it's casually laid on a chair in a room he is in regularly.

1

Have a pocket of really good-but-tiny treats with you. Then the trick is to get the parka associated with something good. This takes patience and excellent timing.

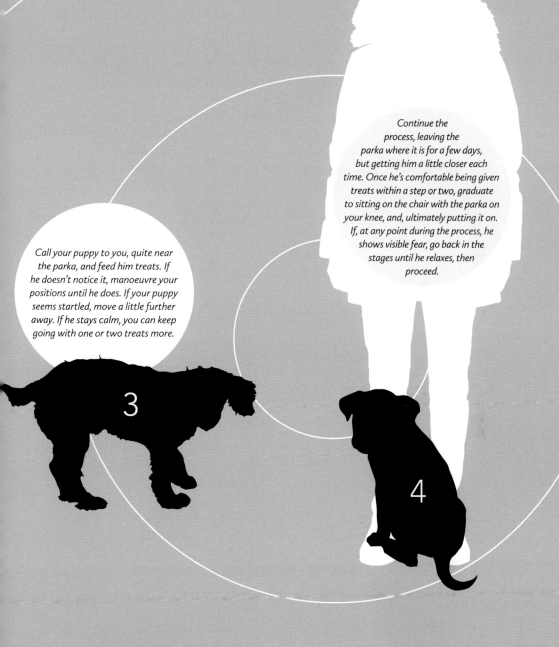

Call your puppy to you, quite near the parka, and feed him treats. If he doesn't notice it, manoeuvre your positions until he does. If your puppy seems startled, move a little further away. If he stays calm, you can keep going with one or two treats more.

Continue the process, leaving the parka where it is for a few days, but getting him a little closer each time. Once he's comfortable being given treats within a step or two, graduate to sitting on the chair with the parka on your knee, and, ultimately putting it on. If, at any point during the process, he shows visible fear, go back in the stages until he relaxes, then proceed.

3

4

MAKING
FRIENDS

When, at 12 weeks, your puppy has had his final vaccination, he can finally go anywhere and mix with all other dogs without you worrying about any possible infections. Remember, though, that there isn't a one-size-fits-all answer when it comes to socialization. A relatively timid puppy may enjoy one-to-one playdates with a matched puppy of similar age, while an all-out-sociable puppy may appreciate a large group of different dogs to play with (the kind of group you find at dog-walking hotspots in parks everywhere).

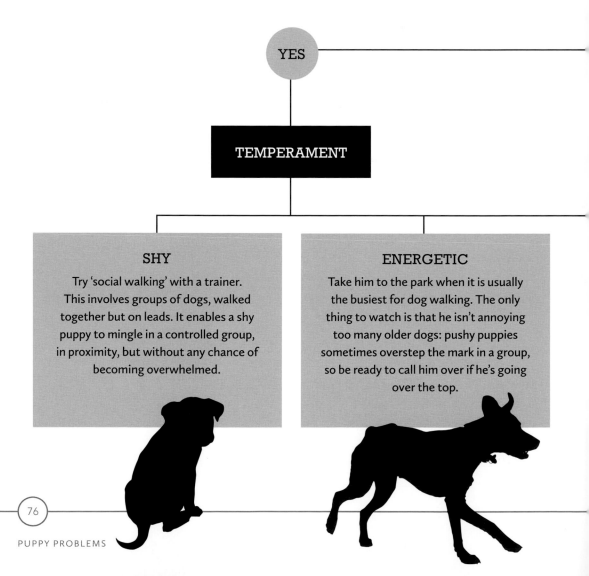

YES

TEMPERAMENT

SHY

Try 'social walking' with a trainer. This involves groups of dogs, walked together but on leads. It enables a shy puppy to mingle in a controlled group, in proximity, but without any chance of becoming overwhelmed.

ENERGETIC

Take him to the park when it is usually the busiest for dog walking. The only thing to watch is that he isn't annoying too many older dogs: pushy puppies sometimes overstep the mark in a group, so be ready to call him over if he's going over the top.

PERSONALITY

It's desirable that puppies are socialized with lots of different dogs in lots of different circumstances – even if he has two or three close canine friends, he should also have a wider acquaintance to give him the chance to navigate plenty of different sorts of canine personalities. But there are several ways of doing this, so make sure you pick the one that best suits your puppy.

DOG'S-EYE VIEW

PLAY ETIQUETTE

I love playing with humans, but given the chance, I enjoy playing with other dogs just as much – or even more. I meet all kinds of different dogs, both breeds and personalities, at the dog park, and I like to invite all of them to play. Most accept, although there's the occasional antisocial type who declines. My human sensibly leaves me to manage my own play relationships on the whole. She knows that playing can sound quite growly without being scary for me, but she still keeps an eye on things.

VACCINATED?

NO

STAY AT HOME
He cannot go for walks in the wider world yet

CALM

Safely enclosed fields are available for hire by the hour in many areas if you want your puppy to run around freely in a few acres with one or two friends. Build a select group to play together by setting a regular time and inviting park or puppy party friends to join in.

FOR ANY AND ALL

Try training and activity classes. Most puppies will benefit from a general training class, where they'll get to mix with a variety of dogs in a controlled environment. It's not free play, but there are enough activities and learning exercises to give you an idea of whether they'll enjoy other classes.

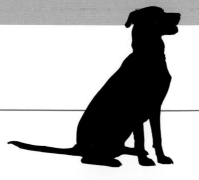

CHAPTER THREE

HEADING FOR
ADOLESCENCE

By the time he's four months old, your puppy will be well settled in at home and used to his routine. Over the next two or three months, you'll notice how quickly he is growing – and growing up – although the timing of his growth spurts will depend a lot on what breed he is. He'll get taller before he fills out, giving him that recognizably gangly older-puppy look, and, as he hits adolescence at around six months, he may start to test the boundaries and try your patience, just as a human teenager would. His social life, both with dogs and people, will probably be widening, too, and he will need even more exercise to wear him out, and training to keep his manners on track.

DEAL
BREAKERS

Most people know that adolescents can be very testing indeed, and this may apply as much to the canine as to the human variety. The period between six months and one year plus is often the most taxing one for an owner as they watch their cute wriggly puppy turn into a smart and often opinionated teenager. It's not invariable: some puppies sail through adolescence cheerfully and problem-free. The majority, though, will present at least some challenges. Careful attention, affection and training are your way through the teenage months, and will help you survive with your bond strengthened and your sense of humour intact.

▼ Second puppyhood

Some owners find the 'teenage' months the most testing of all when it comes to getting their puppy to do what they want. This stage is worth an investment of energy in both training and playing with your puppy – and even the later developers will eventually grow up.

KEEPING UP

Training really helps – not only does it reinforce what is and isn't acceptable behaviour in your puppy's increasingly independent mind, but spending dedicated time together also helps to reinforce the bond between you – and continues to underline the fact that you're the person in charge, and the source of all the good things – food, fun, treats and walks. In one revealing, though depressing, study carried out into rescue dogs in the US, it was found that around 70 per cent of dogs given up to shelters were either adolescents or young adults – between seven to eight months and two years – and that, of those given up, only three per cent had been given any training at all.

Those results seem to indicate that, first, many owners hadn't given enough thought to how big a commitment a dog would be, and, second, that without doing any training with their puppy, they became increasingly unable to cope with more demanding behaviour from a maturing dog as he hit adolescence and beyond. Training does take commitment, but once it's become a habit, it's not difficult: consistency and daily sessions are far more important than spending huge amounts of time at it. Increasing the amount of exercise he gets – and sometimes changing its nature (agility courses or flyball, for example) can make a huge difference to 'challenging' teenage canines too.

▼ **Let him take his time**
Your dog will grow up at his own
rate, and there's no way of hurrying
the process. If you can, view him
and his behaviour objectively and
respond to what he's actually doing
rather than thinking about the stage
he 'should' be at.

PERSONALITY TRUMPS BREED

There are no hard-and-fast rules when it comes to how long adolescence lasts. You've probably heard that
small dogs grow up faster than big ones. To an extent, that's true; breeds mature at different rates, and
while a small terrier might hit adolescence at six months and be considered an adult at a year old, a Labrador
may turn teenage a little later – at perhaps eight months – and only really get to 'grown up' status when he's
two, or even a little older. Generally, if a large dog still has that look of having to grow into his paws, he's not
quite there yet, but most owners will reference behaviour ahead of appearance – some breeds are known
for energetic and puppy-like behaviour well into their technical adulthood. And of course, your dog is also
an individual – there are plenty of calm, chilled examples of breeds with high-energy reputations, just as
there are excitable dogs from breeds that are famous for being laid back.

BROADER HORIZONS

Adolescent dogs, male and female, are suddenly much more interested in the wider world. They are maturing sexually, so they're instinctively looking for a mate; they're flooded with hormones, and their confidence has also grown, so they're inclined to be more assertive.

USE YOUR IMAGINATION

Owners are often told that this is the time when they have to make themselves more interesting to their puppy than anything else around him – which is a tall order. A newly sexualized and highly energetic dog is unlikely to find walking with you more interesting than investigating a group of unknown dogs in the park, so owners have to be imaginative when it comes to engaging with their newly independent pets.

▼ Mingling
You'll find that canine playdates will usually do a better job of tiring your adolescent puppy out than you can manage yourself.

FIVE SIGNS THAT YOUR PUPPY IS NOW AN ADOLESCENT

- His house-training may start to slip.
- He may seem to forget even the simplest training.
- His concentration is suddenly all over he place.
- His play – particularly with other dogs – seems to have a newly competitive edge, with a lot of leg-over-shoulder posturing and barging.
- He's begun mounting (both male and female dogs will mount; it's by no means confined to males).

SEXUAL MATURITY

Most female puppies come into their first heat aged between six and nine months, while male ones will have a strong surge of testosterone at around six months. Outward signs that this has hit will include your puppy starting to lift his leg when he pees, and 'marking'. This is peeing in small amounts to leave his scent in specific locations.

SHOULD YOU SPAY/NEUTER YOUR PUPPY?

Unless you want to breed from your puppy, spaying or neutering is generally regarded as the sensible option. Most vets recommend that operations are done when puppies are about six months old, or sometimes a little older in the cases of very large, slow-maturing breeds. Some still recommend that a bitch puppy has one season before being spayed (the theory is that it allows the puppy to mature a little, and that if spayed too young, she may become set in slightly 'juvenile' behaviour), others think that spaying before she has a season is preferable. Talk to your vet about what is involved and when it's best done. Dogs will recover from neutering in about a week; bitches take around two weeks to recover from being spayed, and need to be supervised to ensure they don't over-exert themselves.

IS IT TRUE THAT…?

Many myths still float around the whole subject of neutering, but they are just that, myths: a neutered dog doesn't put on weight (unless they're fed too much and don't get enough exercise), nor does his or her personality change, although a bitch will avoid the hormonal ups and downs involved with coming into season, and a male dog won't frantically hunt after smelling a bitch who is in season. For a long time it was believed that neutering would also reduce aggression in dogs; recent research, though, shows that the two are usually unconnected.

On the plus side, there are definite health benefits – dogs can't get testicular cancer, and the risks of a bitch developing breast cancer are greatly reduced.

▲ **Hormones kick in**
With some female puppies, you may not see many signs that she is growing up before she has her first season. If you decide to go ahead and let her mature a bit more before spaying, but don't intend for her to have a litter, be ready to keep her away from a lot of male dogs' strong interest.

GETTING INTO
GOOD HABITS

While it may be a slight blow to find that you're no longer the centre of your maturing puppy's universe, there are some straightforward ways to help you manage his newfound independence.

REINFORCING THE GOOD STUFF

If you became slightly more relaxed about training as your puppy seemed to be happily falling in line at around the four- to five-month point, his adolescence is a reminder to get back on it, and to be extremely conscientious about spending dedicated time with him every single day. Keep to a routine of plenty of exercise and if he's going through a forgetful phase, practise things he knows well – even if you end up rewarding him for a simple sit five times running.

Now that he's old enough to 'earn' his privileges, make sure everything is done on a swap principle – that is, he has to do something for you before you do something for him. Nothing should come for free. Ensure that he sits for his meals and before you play with him.

▼ Quid pro quo
The principle of swapping benefits with your puppy, rather than giving him something for nothing, will help reinforce your 'benevolent leader' role. Even little things, like ensuring he sits before his dinner bowl is put down, will help him remember who's in charge.

PUPPY PROBLEMS

It's now, too, that 'Watch me' (see pages 56–57) comes into its own. When you're out with him and dealing with many distractions, knowing that you have a habitual cue that will get his attention is invaluable. (And if practice on this one had slipped, reinstate it and make sure that you practise it daily, in as many different and distracting places as you can.) Is he desperate to sniff at a particular corner that's just a few steps off route? Make him 'Watch me', and, when he does, allow the diversion. Does he want a meet-and-greet with that dog over there? Make him 'Watch me' and sit, and as soon as he does, let him head off. The rule is that he gets to do what he wants to do only after he's checked in with you.

▲ A wider world

Quick, random practice of 'Watch me!' becomes more useful than ever as an increasingly independent dog is getting out and about, and enjoying lots of new experiences.

EATING AND
CHEWING AGAIN

Your puppy was probably eating four meals a day until he was three months old, and then three meals until he hit the six-month milestone. At some point after six months and before he's a year old, he can go down to two larger meals a day, and most dogs stay on two meals daily for the rest of their lives.

WHAT SHOULD YOU FEED AN OLDER PUPPY?

By the time he reaches six months, your puppy will usually be around three-quarters of his adult size. Most puppies should continue to eat their 'puppy' diet, which is higher in protein and calcium – and calories – until they're around three-quarters their adult size (see page 26), when they can switch to their adult diet. A number of specific large breeds – including giant dogs, such as Great Danes or St Bernards – and some that have a propensity for problems such as hip dysplasia – such as German Shepherds – will need a particular diet that balances calcium and protein until they are fully grown. This is to stop 'spurts' in bone growth that may compromise their bone and joint strength as adults.

PLAY WITH YOUR FOOD

If you feed your puppy dry food or kibble, you can make him work for some or all of his meal by scattering it on the floor rather than putting it in a bowl (on a fine day, you can scatter it in the garden). It will take him longer to find and eat, and most dogs enjoy this. If he's fed 'wet' food, you can give him an equivalent workout by stuffing some of his meal into a Kong toy and freezing it. Again, it will take him some time to get the food out.

▼ Tough enough to chew
Many adolescent puppies seem to find rope toys particularly satisfying chews. Buy sturdy plaited ones so that they won't be reduced to handfuls of stringy pieces by increasingly strong teeth.

CHEWING FOR GROWN-UPS

You might have presumed that once his adult teeth were all present, your puppy's chewing needs would be reduced. You'd be mistaken: the new teeth need plenty of workouts, and are substantially more powerful than his puppy set, so it's particularly important that he doesn't get hold of anything you don't want him to have. Where puppy teeth might have left small gnaw-marks on a pair of shoes, for example, his adult set will quickly reduce them to pieces. Dogs also like variety in what they chew, so it's sensible to invest in a good range of chewables, including some very long-lasting and tough ones. Keep them 'fresh', and your puppy interested, by having only a couple out at any one time, and changing them around daily. They could include bones, rawhide chews of different sizes and shapes, and hard rubber Kong toys.

▲ Rawhides
The smaller rawhide 'cigar' chews will easily be eaten in one session; the larger, multi-layered ones will take longer to devour.

CHEW TIME

In the wild, a dog would get his chewing workout along with his meal, eating whole prey animals, bones and all. That's what his teeth have evolved to do, but today, unless you feed your puppy a BARF – bones and raw food – diet, he will gulp his food (dogs don't chew when what they're given is already in manageable pieces) and must fulfil his chewing needs separately.

THE SECOND
FEAR STAGE

The second fear stage (or, to give it its formal name, the 'fear imprint period') is a rather amorphous thing. While the first fear stage is neatly placed on a puppy's timeline at between eight and 10 weeks, some puppies don't seem to experience a second one at all, and while most trainers and behaviourists believe that it exists, the time frame is much longer. It may strike at any point after your puppy is six months old and any episodes are usually over by the time he reaches 14 months.

WHAT HAPPENS?

During this second fear stage, your puppy may go through short periods (usually lasting for between one and three weeks, and usually only once or twice), when he exhibits a high state of 'startle' and fear, sometimes in reaction to things that are new to him, sometimes to familiar things that he's taken no notice of for months previously, and sometimes (as far as can be seen by the human eye, anyway) to nothing at all. As his owner, you may find it disconcerting when your puppy, who's seemed overall to be growing in confidence, is suddenly and unexpectedly spooked, especially when it's by something you thought was familiar to him.

WHY DOES IT HAPPEN?

A number of theories have been developed around this: just as the first fear period comes along at about the time a wild dog pup would begin to explore outside the den, so the second stage seems to coincide with the age at which a fast-growing puppy headed towards adulthood would be wandering much further afield.

An exaggerated fear reflex may have developed to guard him from the unfamiliar – we know that someone putting up their umbrella on an urban street poses no threat to our puppy, but he may be reacting to it with an impulse that originally warned him that, say, a hyena was not a potential friend: it's an old reaction in a contemporary situation.

▼ **Expect the unexpected**
It can come as a surprise when your confident canine teenager suddenly starts to act jumpily. And the second fear stage isn't fully understood by experts. Approach his fears in the same way you did when he was a smaller puppy, calmly, and without ever coercing him when he's scared.

FROM INSIDE HIS BRAIN

Can his brain process what's happening? Another theory says a second fear stage is an indication that a puppy's life experiences so far haven't been extensive enough to ensure that the dense network of neurons and the connections between them in his brain have developed to their greatest potential. In a growing mammal, every new experience prompts new connections in the brain, which, in response, becomes ever more capable of coping with a huge range of situations. In a puppy with a smaller range of experiences, the connections may not be as numerous, and the reaction from the amygdala, the brain's emotional centre, may be fear.

CHAIN REACTION

In many ways a dog's brain is not dissimilar to a human's. The amygdala, deep in the brain, is the place where the fear impulse is generated, while the hypothalamus prompts the release of hormones that are appropriate to how your puppy is feeling – for example, the response to fear may be to release adrenaline, the oft-cited 'fight or flight' hormone. The thalamus helps to focus the brain, dealing with the most important issue of the moment – at stressful moments, it will send information directly to the amygdala, enabling a speedy reaction.

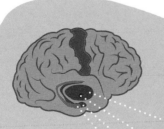

THALAMUS

HYPOTHAMALUS

AMYGDALA

HIPPOCAMPUS

89

▶ New fears

Sometimes old concerns raise their heads again during the second fear stage, but sometimes new ones also turn up. For example, an older puppy who's been calmly watching you vacuum for months may suddenly 'decide' that he hates the noise. Try to overcome such new worries, rather than just shutting him away from the cause.

WHAT SHOULD YOU DO ABOUT IT?

If your fast-growing puppy is evidently frightened, the first thing to do is the same as when he was smaller – calmly take him away from whatever is causing the fear. The fact that he is older doesn't make any difference to how he's experiencing fear, so don't be tempted to 'show' him that there's nothing to be frightened of by taking him closer.

The technique described on pages 72–75 is called counter-conditioning: it works by gradually building positive associations with a person or object that's frightening until it doesn't scare him any more. If you want to help your older puppy to get over his fear in this way, the most important thing is to keep him 'under threshold' while you're working with him. That is, he must be far enough away from the object of his fear not to be reacting to it at all when you begin. If he's already frightened when you start, the positive aspect (being fed treats) won't work. The other key thing is to take things very, very slowly – he must be below threshold the entire time you're working with him, and this means that it may take a lot of sessions to get results.

WHEN WAS HE BORN?

It's not a question that sounds immediately relevant, but the season in which your puppy was born in may offer clues as to why some specifics frighten him now. Even if you were careful to socialize him widely while he was still small, he may not have seen some things simply because it was high summer or the depths of winter and they weren't around – it may be only now that he is seeing his first skateboarder, balloon-seller or sunglasses-wearer. However hot you were on his socialization, it's impossible to cover everything, so deal with any specific fears as they arise. And bear in mind that you may never understand the 'why' behind the fear – for example, why a noisy rubbish truck is accepted with perfect calm, while a plastic bag, blown along by a breeze, is suddenly scary. Your puppy is entitled to decide what frightens him, and it's your job to help him feel calmer about it.

SEASONAL SCARES

Depending on his birth season, your puppy may be reacting to things that are new to him as the seasons change and he's into unfamiliar weather, new kinds of clothes and accessories on 'his' people, and so on. If he was a deep-winter puppy, the screechy scrape of a skateboard, for example, ridden at speed along the street as spring arrives, may scare him simply because he's not heard one before.

BARKING AND
WHAT IT MEANS

Small puppies race around issuing high-pitched yips and yaps. They're amusing to listen to, but a few months down the line, it may come as a surprise when your growing puppy finds his adult bark and uses it. And if he uses it a lot, you may quickly start to wish that he'd stop.

WHY DOES YOUR PUPPY NEED TO BARK?

Because dogs do so much communicating with their body language (and we're so used to telling one another that 'dogs can't talk'), surprisingly little attention has been paid to when and why dogs bark, and what they use barking to 'say'. From the human viewpoint, his bark was one of the original reasons a dog was valuable: he could warn of danger approaching (whether human or animal) long before people had any idea of it. Today, unless you're keeping a dog in very remote country, a tendency towards persistent barking isn't considered to be such a gift; in fact, 'nuisance barking' is a very undesirable trait indeed for anyone with near neighbours.

It's a way to communicate, and, unlike body language, barking can work across distance or if you can't see him. Among the experts who have studied barking, it's a matter of debate whether you can accurately distinguish what different barks 'mean', although most owners will tell you that they can interpret what certain barks mean in certain contexts for their dog.

For example, there's the rapid sequence of barks for when the post arrives (and, as far as the dog is concerned, it always gets results: when barked at, the postal worker goes away), the single, short 'greeting' bark that says hello when a familiar, friendly person arrives, or the single barks with long pauses that are his 'lonely' bark when he's been left on his own. We learn very quickly the idiosyncrasies of our own pet's barks and, in context, we can read them to at least some extent.

▼ **Grown-up barking**
A nuisance barker doesn't develop overnight. Barks are usually used for something, and dogs who end up barking a lot may be bored, lonely or under-occupied. If your canine teenager is suddenly barking a lot, try to identify what's causing it and find a way to redirect his attention to break the habit.

BARKING AND WHAT IT MEANS

WHAT IF HE BARKS TOO MUCH?

It may sound contradictory, but if your puppy shows signs of becoming too keen on barking, it is possible to teach him to start and to stop on cue, although it may take a lot of practice sessions. You need a reliable stimulus that starts him barking – and for most dogs, that will be the doorbell. Because barking is a natural behaviour for dogs, you're not teaching him *how* to do anything, simply *when* to do it – and when to stop.

Begin by teaching him to stop. You'll need some high-value treats for this one, so it's worth having something he really loves as it will have to compete with the attractions of the doorbell, and a friend to ring the doorbell at prearranged time.

▲ **Barking to order**
If he's an enthusiastic barker, you may be able to teach him when to stop as well as to start, although it's a harder trick to teach quieter dogs who don't bark much naturally.

- Your friend will start the sequence by ringing the doorbell. You'll already be standing nearby with your puppy. When it rings and he starts barking, turn to acknowledge the sound of the bell (so that he sees you've registered it – don't go to the door or open it), then turn back to him and hold up a treat. The moment he stops barking, give him the treat.
- If he gobbles the treat but then starts barking again, hold up another treat, wait for him to stop, then give him the treat. Be careful of your timing – you have to give him the treat the second he stops making a noise.
- Repeat three or four times per session. Try to practise every day, and each time leave a very slightly longer gap between the moment he stops barking and the moment that you give him the treat.
- When you can go four seconds between the barking stopping and the treat being given (it's longer than it sounds), you can add the 'Quiet' cue, before he stops barking and as you hold up the treat.
- Barking is a strong impulse in dogs, so practise as often as you can – daily if possible, but at least every two or three days. Gradually apply it in situations where he's barking at other things (maintain a good supply of treats to hand); if you're persistent, you should eventually be able to stop him on cue whenever he barks and you don't want him to.

▲ **Now stop!**
As with any other trick, there needs to be a payoff to get him to fall quiet to order. And your timing needs to be precise so that you don't unwittingly teach him to bark for a treat, rather than to get a treat when he stops barking.

You can also teach him to start barking on cue – although you may not want to use this one so often. To do this, you treat while he's barking – and you have to make sure that the treat is handed over before he's stopped. Again, the timing is critical – he barks, you treat and cue – 'Talk!' – *as* he barks. Again, it can take a while to perfect, but it's good for your teamwork, as he has to understand what you're asking of him, and you have to achieve split-second timing.

A RANGE OF BARKS

Dogs have a wider range of sounds than you may have realized, although some are much more vocal than others, and size and breed may affect the pitch and range of the noises they make. Not as much research has been done into barking as you might expect, given how popular general research into dog behaviour has become in the last decade or so, but the Norwegian author and dog trainer Turid Rugaas has divided the meaning of dog barks into six broad categories: excitement, warning, fear, frustration, guarding and learned barking. The last is the habitual barking of a dog who hasn't been otherwise occupied enough. Remember, these are very basic guidelines – there are plenty of individualists when it comes to barking. Whole books are available on the subject!

FEAR
High-pitched, repetitive, often with a higher 'edge' than a play bark.

FRUSTRATION
High, often rather long noises that may have a whiny edge to them.

WARNING
Sharp, staccato barking, often a short sequence of barks repeated indefinitely (or until the threat goes away).

GUARDING
Lower pitch, often 'gruff' sequence.

EXCITEMENT
High-pitched sequence of barks; often used in play.

LEARNED
The 'nuisance' bark of a dog left too often for long periods. It can develop into almost ceaseless loud, unaccented barking.

DOG-TO-DOG
PLAY

Whole books have been written about how dogs play both with other dogs and with people. Why is it so special? Because it's the sort of behaviour that we rarely get the opportunity to observe in wild animals, but its variations are endlessly fascinating – and in the case of dogs, it takes place on our collective doorstep. There's something in the quality of play too, that can be enjoyed across species; humans may not grab the tug toy between their teeth and relish pulling as hard as they can, but we can imagine just how that feels (which is certainly not the case with all canine habits).

PUPPY PLAY STYLES

Not all animals play, and even when they do, comparatively few play when they are adults, so in the world of animals, dogs – who start to play at around four weeks old and who will often continue all their lives – are the exception, not the rule. And if you empty a group of puppies into a room together, it won't be long before you see a variety of play styles: wrestling, chasing, tug…

Research into puppy groups has shown that not every puppy plays with all the others. Just like in a kindergarten, each has his own preferences; they form into pairs and trios and there are usually one or two who don't seem to have picked up the etiquette of play – perhaps because they've been inadequately socialized and don't speak fluent 'dog'; possibly because they are naturally shyer and feel less able to risk play.

What about your own puppy? If he was socialized with plenty of other dogs before he was 16 weeks old, he's likely to be comfortable playing with a range of ages and types of other dogs, and will quickly establish whether another puppy or adult will play in a way he enjoys. If he's one of the shyer ones, aim to arrange play dates for him with dogs who are known to be friendly – it will be less intimidating for him than expecting him to sort out his own introductions in a park full of dogs. When he's had successful play sessions with two or three dogs without having to cope with a crowd, he's likely to get a taste for it.

▲ **Swapping resources**
Cooperative, relaxed dogs will often share even treasured toys during play sessions: the game is more important than keeping 'their' possessions to themselves.

WHAT NICE PLAY LOOKS LIKE

Can you recognize a game in which both the participants are enjoying themselves? Do you find that you worry that you may not be able to tell if play is going over the top? Even quite young puppies can produce some fearsome play growls and tooth displays when they're intensely involved in a game, and play can look quite rough.

Dogs sign very effectively during play, though, and their body language is so skilled that even humans can often tell what's going on. The more you watch dogs at play, the more accurately you will be able to read the situation and judge whether a player is getting too aroused, and a play scrimmage may be about to turn into the real thing.

DOG'S-EYE VIEW

THE FEEL-GOOD FACTOR

I know how much I enjoy playing, but not really why – various studies, though, have shown that play triggers the production of 'play chemicals': hormones and endorphins that not only make me feel good, but also ensure that I stay relaxed and am extra-receptive to learning as I play. Regular play sessions apparently also reduce my body's production of the hormone cortisol, resulting in lower stress levels – not only while I'm playing, but all the time.

SPOTTING
THE SIGNS

HAPPY PLAY

▲ **Happy face**
The faces of playing dogs' have happy, 'squinty' eyes, and their mouths are usually held open, even when there are a lot of teeth on display. Tongues loll loosely.

▲ **Good play**
The game has constant pauses for a second or two, often marked by play bows (when the 'inviting' dog places his paws flat on the ground, rump in the air) before the players re-engage.

▲ **Relaxed body language**
Tails are loose and flowing.

▲ **Taking turns**
In a chase game, the players are visibly well matched (some dogs will self-handicap, even if they're faster than the dog they're with, in order to let the game continue).

WARNING SIGNS

▲ Overly focused
A dog's face has become very strongly focused, with narrowed eyes.

▲ Tight mouth
The corners of his mouth (the commissure) are tightening into wrinkles. His mouth may be nearly closed and the upper lip is wrinkling.

▲ Still, tense body
Posture has become overly still and tense, and there are fewer pauses and changes of direction in the game.

▲ Tense tail
Tails might be held still, upright and tense (or, in the case of a fearful dog, held low or even tucked between the back legs).

▲ Failure to share
One dog is 'winning': catching up and overtaking, taking the tug toy and not re-offering it. In extreme cases, the loose barging that is part of energetic play may transform into body slamming.

STOP PLAY

Don't hesitate to stop a game if you see any of the danger signs, or even if there's a sense of increasing tension about it – most people who are used to watching dogs together are likely to have 'just a feeling' before the more serious signs (for example, closed mouth/hard stare combinations) manifest themselves. You can break up a 'game' that's not going well by walking towards the players, clapping your hands, and shouting something short and sharp 'Hey!' The dogs will call a halt and refocus on you (call them to you, ask for sits and treat to refocus them) – and you can judge whether they can return to playing after a minute or two's break.

PERSON-TO-DOG
PLAY

The ideal way for you to interact with your dog is with a mixture of physical activity and mental stimulation. As your puppy's energy levels seemingly go up and up, you'll also want to give him the sort of exercise that will leave him thoroughly tired out. Be careful though. At under a year (up to 18 months or two years for large and giant breeds), too much or too violent exercise is a problem for puppies. This is because a puppy has soft layers of cartilage, called growth plates, at the ends of each bone, which cushion it from harm. If the growth plates are damaged, it can cause the puppy's growing bones to distort to accommodate the problem, and give him joint and skeletal problems in adulthood.

GO CAREFULLY

This means that exercise must be moderate. While in dog-to-dog play, puppies largely seem to know their limits, even when they're playing very hard, but they seem to be less aware when it comes to playing throw games with a person, so you need to call the shots. You shouldn't encourage a puppy under a year old to jump, twist or over-exercise to the point of exhaustion – so very active frisbee sessions or full, adult classes in agility or flyball, for example, are out. If you'd like your puppy to attend some kind of exercise class,

▲ Don't overdo it
Games are fun for both of you, but don't overdo it while he's still growing – play energetically, but don't go over the top.

training classes that are designed to accommodate soft puppy
joints exist, offering agility courses that are carefully put together,
with the aim of preparing young dogs for the day when they can
train as the next agility or flyball champion. Seek them out at your
local dog club or training class – they're usually called pre-agility or
sports foundation classes. Ordinary training classes are excellent
for all-round socialization, too (for owners as well as dogs; it's
useful to have the chance to 'talk dog' with other owners and to
set up social walks) and most offer the chance for a bit of play for
your puppy thrown in. Go along to the initial session and check
that only positive and kind training techniques are used before
you sign up.

BRAIN GAMES

Outside classes and broader social situations, you can go the
thinking route. Puppies (in fact, dogs generally) find learning a new
trick or figuring out a game quite as tiring as tearing around a field
with their friends, so concentrate on the mental stimulation part of
the equation.

▼ **Working it out**
You'll find that teaching him a trick
or getting him to figure out where
you've hidden a favourite toy will
engage his interest; it's good to give
him a brain workout every so often.

PERSON-TO-DOG PLAY

▼ Lay a treat trail

A trail of hidden treats, either in the garden or inside – if there's a room or two where you don't mind things getting ruffled up a bit – is good fun. When he's used to the idea, you can hide them in increasingly challenging spots.

TREAT-HUNTING

Improvise toys and games based on food hunts. Treat trails can start simple and get more complex as he becomes used to hunting out the treats. Cardboard is great for a quick home-made game and is usually easy to find around the house. Never recycle cardboard boxes or tubes without getting a game out of them first; use them, instead, to conceal treats – from folding a couple into a small cardboard tube (they're surprisingly hard for a puppy to unfold without a valuable minute or two of paw-and-tooth concentration) to concealing a few in a large boxful of packing paper and card for a longer-lasting hunt.

You can also buy or make a snuffle mat. This is a mat covered with a thick layer of fabric strips. To use it, you scatter kibble or treats among the strips, shake the mat so they settle at the base of the fabric, and let your puppy hunt and snuffle them out. Don't leave the mat out after the treats have all been found, or your puppy will start to chew on the fabric: put it away until next time. It can also be used to feed your dog part of his meal – it makes a slower version of the play-with-your-food idea.

TUG OF WAR AND KILL-THE-TOY

One of the reasons that puppies enjoy playing with each other so much is that they're equally enthusiastic about the game. And in the same way, playing is more fun for your dog if you join in with as much enthusiasm as he shows. Hide his tug toy or his stuffed squeaky animal and 'hunt' for them with him before having a game, or tie it to the end of a string and have it move, apparently of its own volition, just as he's going to fetch it, so that he has to chase after it around and under things.

DIGGING

Some puppies are inveterate diggers from a very young age. Usually it's down to their breed: terriers, for example, have been bred to dig for generations – it can be hard to train out of them, so work with them rather than against them and give them a digging place (this can be a child's sandpit or a remote area of the garden where a patch of ground can be given over to his hobby. You can then play a regular 'buried treasure' game with him – hide a favourite toy or a wrapped treat and start digging along with him until he gets the idea and is happy to go solo.

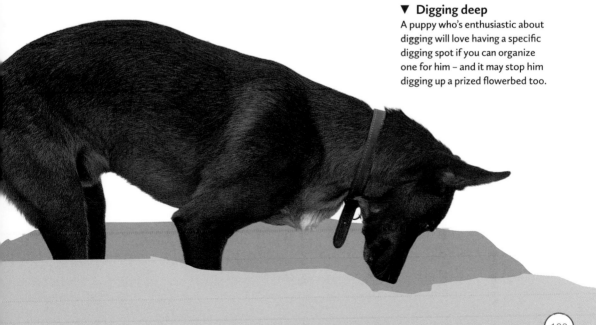

▼ Digging deep
A puppy who's enthusiastic about digging will love having a specific digging spot if you can organize one for him – and it may stop him digging up a prized flowerbed too.

PERSON-TO-DOG PLAY

CHAPTER FOUR

IN IT FOR
THE LONG HAUL

By the time he's reached around nine months old, your puppy is well on

the way to adulthood. He may still be acting like a teenager but, if you've

put the work in, he'll already have a good foundation to build on. Even if

he sometimes has a moment of adolescent rebellion and seems to forget

the rules, you'll have helped him to acquire most of the skills he'll need

for your future life together. From this point on, you can keep practising

anything he hasn't quite familiarized himself with, maintain his key skills –

particularly recall and all-round socialization – and enjoy his company.

ADDING IT UP:
WHERE YOU ARE

You're probably well aware of the things that still need work where your puppy's concerned. What you may be less conscious of is where you might need some help. If he could, what would your puppy tell you about your training technique?

FIVE MISTAKES ALMOST ALL HUMANS MAKE WHEN THEY'RE TRAINING

1 *You talk too much*
Limit yourself to body language and short cues – 'Watch me', 'Come' and so on. Far too many dogs are used to hearing 'Rex, come! Come here! Come over here now! Rex, get over here...' and so on. Remember, he doesn't speak English.

2 *You repeat yourself*
Two times is enough for most cues (see above). If you've asked him twice, using just the cue words, and he's ignored you twice, you need to think of another way to do it.

◀ **Still listening**
Even young dogs have an impressive ability to keep listening and trying to work it out – even when they're muddled about what you want of them.

▶ **Time for a break**
If your puppy is yawning a lot, tongue-flicking, or beginning to become evidently distracted, it's probably time for a break: the training session may have been going on too long.

TRY, TRY AND TRY AGAIN

However exasperating you sometimes are to me, with your incessant talking and your confusing instructions, I'll always keep working, trying to figure out what you mean. By now, I understand that you are management and that it benefits me all round when I keep up with what you want. To be honest, I think I'm better at this try, try, try again business than you humans are.

3 *You don't give him time to think*
Let him think about whether he's going to do what you've asked. Not for ages, but for a second or two. The human tendency is to leave hardly any time between the first and the second time of asking – and it's better to let your dog think about it and decide that he's going to go along with your ideas. If you find it impossible to wait and be still, do something positive with your body language – for example, if you asked him to come and he hasn't yet, clap your hands or slap your leg: at least you won't be repeating yourself.

4 *You don't train often enough*
Most people are keen to train their small and malleable puppy at the beginning. But as the novelty wears off, and the problem areas start to show (and even the fastest-learning puppy usually has difficulty picking up one or two things), training tends to become less regular. Every day, ideally two or three sessions, is best. But...

5 *...You spend too long training*
Training sessions – things your puppy needs to know – are best interleaved with play sessions – things your puppy enjoys doing – until the two are almost interchangeable in his mind. No dog enjoys lengthy periods of serious instruction; hardly any dog, though, doesn't love a game of tug followed by a minute or two of amply rewarded 'Watch me!'

If you've got out of the habit of several-times-daily sessions, the human tendency is to compensate by making less-frequent sessions longer. Resist it: overlong sessions will bore your puppy and make you tense. Keep them short, with plenty of breaks for play.

KEEPING UP
TRAINING

You can attend a specific training class, such as those that teach the Kennel Club's Good Citizen scheme (see page 115), which will be helpful both for your puppy's socialization and to help him learn things such as a prolonged 'Stay'. But in a broader, more everyday sense, training needs to carry on throughout your dog's life, whatever else is going on. Whether he's proving easy or hard, quick or slow to train, never assume that, because you've taken huge pains to ensure that he has a good recall now, it will remain intact in two years' time if you and he haven't continued to practise it.

MAKING IT FRESH

Remember to keep asking your dog for a few specifics – in particular, to 'Come' to ensure that his recall stays sharp. As you settle into a routine with a nearly-adult dog, exercise and play tend to take precedence over training. But play naturally builds in training behaviour: after all, there's no point playing fetch with a dog who refuses to give up the ball. Ask for a sit before you throw it again, call your puppy to 'Come' when he's just collected the frisbee ready for another go. His training will be reinforced without him even realizing it.

◄ **Mix it up**
You can keep things varied for your puppy by mixing 'formal' training – maintaining a reliable recall, for example – with brain games or trick training. The variety should help to keep him interested.

▲ Keeping his attention

Engaging your puppy's attention becomes even more important as he's growing up and getting more independent. Always use a spare minute or two to practise with him, even if it's just a simple 'Sit' or 'Down'.

DOG'S-EYE VIEW

EASY WINS

Asking me to do something I know well and can do easily builds my confidence. That's why, if you're trying to teach me something that I'm finding difficult, you can help me by asking me for a 'Sit' (the first – and easiest – thing you ever taught me). I don't work so very differently from you in this way: imagine if you were given a difficult equation that you couldn't solve, for instance, wouldn't you feel relieved if it was taken away and you were given a simple addition problem instead? So at moments when you're trying to teach me something complicated and I'm getting frustrated, ask me to do something I can manage easily before we finish the session. It'll pay off in the long term.

YOUNG DOG,
NEW TRICKS

Young dogs have so much energy that giving them plenty of physical exercise tends to take priority. Don't forget that mind games can give dogs' brains a workout too. And if you find that he's a natural, don't dismiss the idea of teaching him some simple party tricks (a rollover, perhaps, or playing dead) that he can use to entertain a human audience: some dogs are natural performers and will enjoy a round of (human) applause.

SIMPLE MIND WORKOUTS

Mind workouts for young dogs are simple to arrange; he'll be happy to work for treats and toys if the hunt is presented in an appealing enough way. You've probably laid a treat trail for him at some point – if not, all you have to do is go into a room where he's not present (and where you're not going to mind him doing a lot of digging or snuffling about), and hide a handful of treats, some in straightforward places, others in slightly harder ones. Then you go into the room with him, ask him 'Where's the treat?' (with plenty of high-pitched excitement) and watch him nose them out. As he gets used to the routine, you can hide them in increasingly difficult

▼ **Play dates**
If your puppy is a solo dog at home, organizing play dates with friends' pets will build on his socialization, and organizing a joint game or activity will help too.

WHAT YOU TEACH ME

Do I mind what tricks or games we play? Not particularly; as long as I'm happily occupied, I live in the moment. Don't forget that there are a whole range of human concerns I don't have any idea of. When your human friend criticized you for teaching me tricks because they were 'undignified', I didn't know what he meant (I don't have any concept of what 'dignity' means, to be honest). If you want to teach me something that I'm going to like learning – like the 'Play dead' trick – feel free. We'll both be enjoying ourselves.

◀ End game

A game is always as good or better than a treat as a payoff at the end of a workout/training session, and will help to use up any leftover energy too.

places so that he has to follow his nose and then work out how best to access them. In good weather, a treat trail laid outside will be even more interesting to him, as the natural range of outdoor smells will be competing with the treats.

Similarly, you can hunt-the-toy with your puppy's favourite tug toy, or frisbee or ball. Start with easy spots, reward every 'find' with a quick game, then hide it again somewhere a little harder. (Don't forget that dogs have an inability to distinguish between red and green, so toys in those colours will be harder for him to find amongst greenery – if you want to play fetch, choose a blue or yellow ball or a throw toy instead).

PLAYING TO THE AUDIENCE:
EASY TRICKS

What about tricks? Both rolling over and lying flat – 'Play dead' – are easy to teach, as you can lure him into the right position with treats. Then all he has to do is link a couple of steps together for himself (trainers call this ability 'chaining'.)

Once he's got the idea, you may find that it's hard to stop him 'performing' in the hope of an additional reward.

If your dog likes treats, luring him into a rollover won't take long. Take your time over the second step before going on to the third.

1

To train your puppy to rollover, ask him for a 'Down' or lure him into one with a treat.

Take another treat and hold it near his nose, then use it to lead his nose over his shoulder so that he's lying on his side. Once he's there, give him the treat.

Practise this a few times until he's comfortable with rolling onto his side.

2

'PLAY DEAD'

'Play dead' is even simpler to teach – although for the full 'dead' effect, your puppy needs to lie still for a moment or two at the end of the manoeuvre – which, if he's energetic, may prove the hardest part to teach him.

- Again, start with a 'Down'.
- Take a treat, hold it close to his nose, and guide his nose over his shoulder until he's lying on his side. Give him the treat.
- Take another treat, and use it to lure his head down flat on the floor (so he's lying completely flat, 'playing dead'. Once his head is on the floor, give him the treat.
- Introduce a delay between getting his head flat and giving him the treat so that he lies still for a moment or two.

3

SUMMARY

Go through the steps several times, first breaking to give him a treat at the middle point (when he's lying on his side), then when he completes the roll. After a few sessions, he should be able to complete the roll with the lure of a single treat.

The final step in the chain is to take another treat once he's lying on his side, and use it to encourage him to take his nose over his shoulder again. In the process, he rolls onto his back, then onto his other side – completing the rollover.

MORE
SOCIALIZATION

Ideally while your dog is still young – even if he's strictly passing out of the puppy phase – he should continue to meet lots of other dogs in a variety of circumstances. This isn't the same thing as a regular meet-up with his friends for a play, it's specifically about encountering different sorts of canine characters, from the easy-going to the grumpy, so that as he approaches full-on adulthood, he's as broadly socialized as possible.

YOUR PUPPY'S SOCIAL CIRCLE

Even if a puppy has six best friends he plays with every day, research has shown that, however amiably he gets on with them, having a relatively limited social circle won't necessarily help to make him all-round fluent with other dogs. Some dogs love every dog they meet, others need a little more time and space, still others are very selective indeed. And even if your dog belongs to the first group, it's useful for him to meet representatives of the third, not least so that he can learn that there are other dogs who will prefer him not to get in their faces, greet them too exuberantly or jump on them without a formal introduction. Think of it as an exuberant teenager understanding that his strict grandmother appreciates a more rule-bound way of doing things than comes naturally to him.

MEET AND GREET

There are a number of ways of ensuring that your puppy meets dogs that are new to him. Social walking is one: look online to see if any trainers or owners run a social walk in your area. As you'd assume from the name, these usually involve a group of dogs being taken for a walk together. They're generally kept on their leads, and there may be other activities within the walk that they'll enjoy, such as treat hunts or gentle trick training. Many owners with less-than-fully socialized dogs use them to help their pets get used to others, so even if your puppy is a social butterfly, he's likely to meet a range of canine personalities safely and without stress.

▼ **Class advantage**
One of the major pros of training classes is that they help you to spot any potential socialization problems – maybe you have a large-breed puppy who seems nervous of smaller dogs, or vice versa? – and provide help to deal with them.

TRAINING CLASSES

If he attended a puppy class and enjoyed it, your puppy might benefit from being enrolled in a regular obedience class that trains dogs to receive their Good Citizen certificates (he may even have already received the basic level certificate, for the puppy foundation course). These courses are Kennel-Club endorsed, and there are three levels to train for – bronze, silver and gold. If your puppy has a tendency to get overexcited in the company of other dogs, these more formal training classes are a good way to accustom him to paying attention to you even in the distracting presence of other dogs, and there will usually be enough time and opportunity for him to meet and socialize with the other dogs at the beginning and end of the classes. Some very sensitive puppies may feel overloaded by the combination of lots of other unknown dogs and the need to concentrate on training, but for most, classes work well on both the socialization and the training fronts.

DOG'S-EYE VIEW

SIGNS OF FRIENDSHIP

We dogs have just as many likes and dislikes as humans do when it comes to other members of our own species. Meeting lots of other dogs won't necessarily mean that I make a greater number of friends, but it does help my fluency in speaking 'dog' – the signals I send out – and my ability to read the signals that other dogs send to me, too. In other words, it makes me better at being a dog.

ON THE LEAD /
OFF THE LEAD

Your nearly grown puppy almost qualifies to be called a dog now – so should he be running around off lead all the time? Because they've done plenty of training, and worked hard on their puppy's recall, owners often feel that their dogs should be able to be off the lead wherever they are. Enjoy having him run around, burning off energy, everywhere it's appropriate, but continue to exercise caution – or to follow the middle way of keeping him on a long line when you're not sure. And there are still a few circumstances when your dog should be on the lead regardless of how good his recall is. Sometimes it's because there's a risk to your puppy, while at other times it's about consideration for other people and dogs.

AROUND LIVESTOCK

Circumstances in which your puppy should be on the lead no matter what include times when he's walking amongst (or even in proximity to) livestock. His chase instincts can be surprisingly strong, and, with many instances annually of farm animals being chased, hurt or even killed, farmers rightly take any chasing behaviour very seriously indeed. On the other hand, even owners who had considered their dogs to be cast-iron reliable are often taken off guard by how strong the prey instinct can be, and how uncharacteristic it may seem of any other behaviour they've ever seen in their dog. So keep him on the lead; letting him off in these circumstances is not worth the risk.

▼ Under control

Farmers and riders aren't understanding about off-lead dogs chasing or barking: it's not only anti-social, it can be dangerous. Be persistent when it comes to teaching your puppy to walk quietly and to heel when it's necessary.

PUPPY PROBLEMS

AROUND REACTIVE DOGS

Keep your puppy on the lead, too, if you see other dogs being walked on the lead nearby, even when you're in an off-lead area. The other dog's owner has reasons for keeping their pet on a lead, and it's better (and safer for your own puppy) to respect that. Their dog may be strongly reactive to, or fearful of other dogs – or both. And if you've ever been in charge of a reactive dog yourself, you'll know that the most annoying, or, in a worst-case scenario, frightening, thing that can happen is for another dog to run up to yours, which may be scared, barking or lunging, while their owner shouts from a distance, 'Don't worry, he's friendly!' Avoid being that other owner and either keep or put your puppy on a lead if you're walking close to other on-lead dogs.

IN TOWN

You may have trained him to walk closely to heel and be justifiably proud of your joint achievement. Nevertheless, anywhere where there are pavements and traffic, he should still be on the lead. He may have perfect manners and be prepared to stick to you like glue, but you can't rule out the unexpected when it comes to vehicles, or other people or animals. It's not safe to show off: keep him on the lead.

▼ Leads in town
Even if you drive safely, other drivers may cause a problem. The same goes for dogs: even if you would trust your young dog off-lead on the street, a passing dog may not be so well-behaved or socialized. On-lead is safer.

ON THE LEAD / OFF THE LEAD

HOW TO DEAL WITH
GUARDING

Many dogs are easy-going about their resources – food, toys, sleeping place – and are laid-back enough to eat, play, or sleep whoever else is around. Others are less relaxed, but will tolerate it. Guarding behaviour is perfectly natural, but arises when your dog becomes concerned that the things he values are going to be taken away from him. You may have spotted it when your puppy was younger, but until he was a bit older it may not have seemed like much of a problem. After all, if a tiny puppy gave a tiny growl when you took his toy away, you probably barely noticed it. If you didn't really notice it when he was smaller, or if he's only now showing signs of starting to resource guard his toys or food, you need to deal with it.

SIGNS OF GUARDING

The body language of guarding isn't hard to read: your puppy may go a little stiff when you approach his basket, or a valued toy, or his food bowl while he's eating. If you then moved closer, he may have growled a little; if he was guarding a toy, he may have run off with it to another room. While it may not seem like a particularly big deal – after all, you didn't want the toy anyway – guarding is behaviour that you need to take seriously. If it's only a slight tendency, the following methods will help, but any signs of serious guarding may call for some professional help. Never confront a dog by trying to snatch whatever it is that he's guarding: it's an easy way to get yourself bitten. Instead, try the stealth option – regain control by showing your puppy that having you around is an asset, not a threat.

▼ Watchful
Guarding is easy to spot. Your puppy may become intensely focused on the item he's guarding. His usual easy movements may become still and he may go still as you approach it or him. Treat guarding with respect, as it can be a serious problem.

SWAP

Playing swap can be a good way to deal with possessiveness around toys or other valued objects. It's simply an exchange of an object for one that your puppy will regard as having a higher value. It does mean that you need to have a mental valuation that will match your dog's when it comes to toys – and you need to start with something that he doesn't place much value on. If you tend to have a lot of toys out, put them all away when you're teaching him to swap, so there aren't numerous options for him to choose from. Then, whenever he has an item (left out by you deliberately), you offer him something better. For example, if he's chewing on an old rawhide chew without much gnawing value left in it, offer him a new one as a swap. If he's got a paw on a squeaky toy whose squeak died, offer him the much-newer plush version that still squeaks loudly. And so on. As soon as he's given up the less valuable item, give it back to him (lesson: you give something up and you get it back as well as something better).

▲ Trading up
Giving up a toy, even as a swap, is a leap of faith on a dog's part. Ensure that he gets it back every time: if he knows that he can rely on you not to take his valued possessions and then refuse to give them back, it will reinforce his all-round trust in you.

HOW TO DEAL WITH GUARDING

FOOD GUARDING

If you're in the habit of leaving your puppy's bowl down between meals, start picking it up and putting it away as soon as he's finished eating, and not putting it down again until he's next fed. You can also help to break the guarding association by moving the spot where he's fed – even if it's only to a different corner of the kitchen. One way to help stop a puppy or young dog guarding his food bowl is to put only a small amount of food down at first, then, when he's eaten it, to pick up the empty bowl and put another small amount of food in it, wait till he's eaten it – and so on. That way, the only association he will build with you handling his bowl is that he's going to get more food. If this begins to relax the guarding behaviour, build on it by throwing extra-good treats in the area of his bowl while he's eating, to give him even more positive associations with having you around at mealtimes.

▼ Mealtimes

Guarding behaviour needs to be dealt with, but equally your puppy deserves to eat his supper undisturbed. Have a house rule that, once his food is put down for him, he's left in peace to eat it. When he's finished, take the bowl away until the next meal is due.

▲ **Be fair**
If you have more than one dog, you should still hold the role of benevolent team leader. Pets will usually have some kind of pecking order between themselves, but you should always be in the top spot.

LOOK AT THE HOUSE RULES

If your puppy is showing signs of resource guarding, make sure that he's asked to 'earn' everything you give him. This isn't arduous: it means that every time he wants something from you, he has to do something for you. This could be a 'Sit' before you throw his ball for him, or a 'Down' when you go to the treat cupboard to get his daily chew treat.

WHY DO DOGS GUARD?

It's a very common behaviour that's not completely understood, but it's widely thought to come from a lack of confidence that leads to a dog feeling that the things he values may be taken away (even when this has never happened). So while it might seem counter-intuitive to tighten up house rules in response to it, many behaviourists believe that if you increase your own 'leadership' in response to it, you are actually helping your dog to feel more secure, and that this may help to alleviate the behaviour.

SERIOUS GUARDING

If playing swap with his toys or adding food treats to his mealtimes aren't working, and, more importantly, if you're beginning to find his behaviour in any way intimidating, it may be time to get some professional help. It's important to solve the problem in any case, and especially if you have children around. Don't allow a child to go anywhere near a resource-guarding dog until the problem is solved. This isn't an admission of defeat, but a sensible response. Ask your vet for a referral to a behaviourist, or look at pages 124–25 for guidelines for finding one for yourself.

TEAMWORK AND
AGILITY

By now, you and your puppy should be a team; he looks to you for guidance when he's uncertain, while you enjoy his company, and you both like spending time together. As he grows up, there are a number of other ways you can build on this. For a young, active dog, an agility course may be the best way he can spend time with you and get some exercise.

WHY AGILITY?
It's the best way to work alongside your dog as he thinks through things and gets some exercise. Agility courses, once he's old enough for them, offer both physical and mental challenges: agility (as the name implies), balance and the ability both to slow down and to speed up as the course demands it all get a workout. Plus the owner guides the dog all the way through, so good agility still has an element of teamwork.

FLYBALL
Increasingly considered a competitor to agility as a dog sport, flyball is played in teams. It's fast and very exciting for the dogs, who run down a lane, jumping hurdles as they go, then release a ball from a box with a lever, before returning, over the hurdles, to the starting point. Most dogs who learn to participate love it, and it encourages them to think and act independently (once they're in their lane, it's up to them, without reference to owner, trainer or anyone else, to get results). Is it right for your newly adult dog? It depends. Some owners prefer activities they can share with their pets, building their bond – in which case they'll prefer an agility option – others love the intensity and extreme workout that flyball offers a motivated dog – and think it's the best exercise, both mental and physical, on offer.

SUSPENDED HOOP

Also known as a tyre jump. The height can be altered to suit the jumping dog, but it poses a greater challenge than the more straightforward jumps or hurdles.

A-FRAME

He runs straight to the top and then down the other side. It sometimes takes some practice to stop a dog jumping off halfway up or down the slope.

DOG WALK

Up, over and down. You can ask him for a pause mid-way.

WEAVE POLES

Also known as slalom. He needs to weave through a sequence of upright poles. This may take a few sessions of treats and training for him to master; in agility competitions, the dog must lead with his left shoulder as he starts to weave.

SEESAW

He runs to the centre, rebalances himself as the seesaw tips, then runs down the slope. Should be taken slowly with less confident dogs to ensure they don't fall, or lose their nerve as the seesaw tips.

TUNNEL

The dog simply has to run through – sometimes there's a bend, so he can't see the open end as he enters.

GOING TOO FAR?

Increasingly, professionals are questioning whether the ball obsession that so many dogs develop in response to distance ball chuckers and, in the case of those who practise it, the extreme excitement of flyball, is good for them. This is relatively new: a decade ago, if anyone had asked if chucking a ball for a dog could be a bad thing, no-one would have taken them seriously. But it's been pointed out that if a dog is waiting for someone to throw them a ball, there's actually no interaction with the person, even less so if they're using a chucker, which throws very far and very fast – far more so than if a ball were thrown by hand. Is there such a thing as 'the wrong kind of exercise'? Owners might doubt it, but there's an argument developing among the professionals that there may be. Watch this space.

IF YOU WANT
PROFESSIONAL HELP

If you've been working for a while on a particular – or particularly challenging – aspect of your puppy's behaviour without getting results and it's starting to worry you, there's no shame in calling in some professional advice or help. If you do decide to call in the professionals, though, where should you look? Do you know if you want a trainer or a behaviourist, or what sort of qualifications should you check for. And how can you ensure that you find someone who will understand you, your puppy and the problem – as well as use kind, positive methods to help?

WHAT THE TERMS MEAN

A trainer teaches a dog to perform certain actions (or, in some cases to stop performing them). They might, for example, help you to teach a strong dog to walk more easily on a lead.

A behaviourist looks at the underlying reasons for a dog's behaviour – seeing the behaviour as a symptom rather than the cause – and at ways of modifying that behaviour by changing the way in which a dog feels about a situation. If an adolescent dog has become strongly afraid of strangers, for example, a behaviourist will look at finding practical ways, such as counter-conditioning, to help to reduce his fear and will work on them with him and his owner as a way of solving the problem.

Behaviourists treat a wide range of problems, including the most challenging, such as separation anxiety or fear-based aggression. There are also trainer/behaviourists out there who combine the two roles.

Finding the right person is made trickier by the fact that someone with no formal qualifications can still set up business as a dog trainer or a behaviourist without breaking the law. This means that some very old-fashioned practices linger on in the less-regulated corners of the dog training-and-behaviour world, including punishment-based techniques that have long since been proved to be ineffective as well as inhumane.

▲ **New perspectives**
A good professional trainer or behaviourist will help to give you a new perspective on your puppy's behaviour and will offer coping strategies or solutions to any persistent problems.

However, The Animal Behaviour and Training Council (ABTC), a comparatively new regulatory body, has been working in the UK since 2009 to establish agreed standards for the knowledge and skills needed by trainers and behaviourists. Their recommendation for an Applied Animal Behaviourist is a minimum qualification of a BSc in Animal Behaviour, which means that ABTC behaviourists will have spent at least three years studying the subject.

The ABTC maintains national registers of qualified trainers and behaviourists – and their practitioner organizations, such as the Association of Pet Dog Trainers (APDT) and The Canine Behaviour and Training Society (TCBTS) – so when you're looking for the right person to help you, these will be a good place to start. Any reputable trainer or behaviourist practising now should focus exclusively on positive methods.

It should go without saying, but we'll say it anyway: no reputable practitioner will use physical force or coercion on a dog, nor 'aversives', such as shock collars or pads (not yet illegal in England, although they are now banned in Scotland and Wales, and in many other countries), nor anything that aims to scare the dog into obedience, such as exaggerated yelling or jerked lead corrections.

WORKING WITH YOU

A good practitioner, whether trainer or behaviourist, will pay attention to you as well as to your puppy. Think through any problems and concerns in detail before an appointment so that you can pinpoint and describe apparent triggers that set a behaviour off, contexts in which it arises, how you behave when it does and so on. Expect (and be ready to answer) plenty of questions about what you do, as well as what your puppy does – this isn't intrusive, it's just fact-gathering. Feel free to ask plenty of questions too. The more support you can get, and the more informed you are about a problem or challenge, the easier it will be for you to work cooperatively with your puppy to solve it.

▼ Keep an open mind
You may find that you're really the one who needs to adjust your behaviour. The professionals are usually good at spotting when your dog doesn't actually understand what you want him to do. Successful sessions will reinforce your relationship with your pet.

INDEX

INDEX

ACKNOWLEDGMENTS

With thanks to all the models and their humans:

Tizzy, Olivia and Rob
Roo and Ellie
Edison and Veronika
Bella and Amelia
Snoop and Tanya
Frankie and Chris
Buddy and Ben
Phoebe and Laura
Luna, Ruby and Tabitha

The following images are © Shutterstock images: 12, 39, 43, 52, 53, 54, 55, 63, 91, 116, 117, 123.

How was the book?
Please post your
feedback and photos:
#DogsEyeView

AMMONITE
PRESS

www.ammonitepress.com